GLOSSARY OF TERMS

FOR ANTI-OPPRESSIVE PERSPECTIVES

ON POLICY AND PRACTICE

Second Edition

Bill Lee

Sheila Sammon

Gary Dumbrill

Editors

COMMONACT PRESS

Welcome to the 2014 second edition

Welcome to the new edition of the Glossary. Changes to this edition are a title change from, "glossary of terms for anti-oppressive policy and practice" to, "glossary of terms for anti-oppressive perspectives on policy and practice." This change reflects our position that anti-oppressive practice is not a distinct set of practice or policy writings that can be acquired, but rather a set of perspectives that inform and can transform a wide range of practice and policy writing skills into mechanisms that oppose oppression. We have added many new definitions and a number of revisions to existing ones. As well, all new and revised definitions have been subject to a formal blind peer review process before incorporation into the publication. We hope you enjoy!

Bill Lee, Sheila Sammon & Gary Dumbrill (editors)

If there is no struggle, there is no progress. Those who profess to favour freedom, and yet depreciate agitation, are [those] who want crops without ploughing up the ground. They want rain without thunder and lightening. That struggle might be a moral one; it might be a physical one, but it must be a struggle. Power concedes nothing without a demand. It never did and never will.

- Frederick Douglass

Foreword

Wha hemas, moosmagilth, kwenque Kundoqk, helqkinew, Haisla, Kemano, Kitselas. My English name is Jacquie Green, Killer Whale from the Haisla, Kemano and Kitselas territories. I am a visitor here in the Lekwungun territory and have studied and worked here for the last eleven years.

It is an honour to be invited to write this foreword as it relates to anti-oppressive practice (AOP) emphasizing "social justice" in our varying professional and personal lives. I will write this from my position first and foremost as an Indigenous woman and secondly from the perspective of my experiences within academia, of living, learning and teaching anti-oppressive practice.

I have had the opportunity to develop, implement and teach anti-oppressive practice over the last six years. These experiences have been invaluable, particularly when co-teaching and co-writing with people who also strive to reinforce social justice within academic institutions. In these various processes of development and delivery, my learning continues to grow and shift based on what emerges with my relationships with diverse people and how these relationships have critically enriched my knowledge of AOP.

Since our first year of teaching AOP at the University of Victoria, the language, the philosophies, the values and beliefs of AOP continue to be shaped and reshaped. Perhaps this truly is what anti-oppressive philosophies are: the continued renewal and shape shifting of difference. In the context of anti-oppressive practice, a central concern is an attentiveness to challenge and confront dominant ways of living and learning that marginalize peoples considered "different" from fully participating in our world. As such, anti-oppressive practices provide space to examine the nexus of 'power, privilege and dominance.' It is through these critical examinations that we recognize and work with/against the forced absence and construction of 'other' within dominant theoretical practices and philosophies. Moreover, we begin to see that in the academy there is a persistence of dominant knowledge, which continues to marginalize and silence other forms of practice and knowledge. By continually examining notions of theory, knowledge, and praxis, we are forced to see how dominant educational pedagogy oppresses and marginalizes groups of people. Particularly with the profession of social work, our continued and unrelenting social constructions and social practices of professionalization and professionalism persistently centralize dominant western ways of knowing and living, contributing to the marginalization of other ways of knowing and living.

Within AOP discourse, I have continuously centered 'difference'. In my course outlines, class lectures, and course readings I present themes that begin with knowledge from 'other' and critically explore how we as social workers could work within and through differences. Our vision is to ensure that people we work with could share their accounts and that we could 'hear' what they say. By critically analyzing our skills, we have an opportunity to expand from our head only to include the heart in our practice. This journey to our heart then shows how we as professionals must shift in our practice and how critical it is to nurture and maintain relationships with all groups of people.

What is challenging here is that we have been encouraged to internalize dominant knowledge and languages for so long, that it is somewhat challenging to re-vision theory in the context of disability, queer, or Indigenous perspectives. However, within an AOP context there is much enthusiasm for people who are 'other' to learn notions of confronting dominant perspectives and exploring from a reflective place of family and community what philosophical position is key to informing effective praxis. In essence, AOP is an opportunity for students to re-vision a social work that centres on social justice with a focus on intersectional views in our praxis. Many of us confront these notions of power and dominance continuously by writing, teaching and learning in the context of Indigenous ways.

As I continue to incorporate Indigenous philosophies into the classroom, I see similarities in philosophies of AOP and traditional Indigenous teachings. Among our diverse groups of Indigenous peoples we are taught by our Elders, our ancestors to honor and respect all living things. We learn as young children that the animals, the trees, the water and sky are all intricate parts of our being and that we cannot survive without one another. Another aspect of Indigenous teachings involves philosophies of an ancient tool known as the medicine wheel. In this wheel we see diversity (various colors of the wheel); our life cycle (infant, youth, adult and elder); our four seasons (spring, summer, autumn and winter) and our being (spiritual, emotional, physical and mental). Within these (few) components I have identified, all these elements represent teachings of respect, our well being, and understanding each aspect of our life starting from our infant stage. As you can see, it is critical to understand one's history as a person in and with the elements of learning and living. But we do not stop here: the wheel also teaches us to see and learn the importance and connections between and with the histories of our families, our communities and our territories.

And so it is within anti-oppressive philosophies, we have space here to critically analyze our histories, to examine our identities, our reflective self and then to move on to how these aspects inform our knowledge of praxis. Most importantly in this approach, we have the opportunity to re-vision our praxis. We can if we want to, re-define what social work is and how it could be effective to truly serve social justice.

Through countless relationships with former students, colleagues and especially my children, I thank you all for teaching me values of life. It is your stories and their vision of life that continually informs how I write social justice into my work. I am reminded daily of my place here on mother earth. I am reminded by my children and other children to ensure that in our professionalizing we must continually understand differences and importantly our abilities to work within/through/across difference to enrich our knowledge.

In closing I want to acknowledge my teachers who are my grandmothers and my great grandmothers who taught my parents a Good Life. It is their teachings that inform what anti-oppressive practice is in social work. It is my traditional teachings that bring to the center of my work what social justice truly is. Wha! Aixgwellas!

Kundoqk (Jacquie Green)
Victoria, British Columbia

Acknowledgements

One of the first things that we need to acknowledge is that Anti-Oppressive Social Work does not stand independently. It did not emerge full blown out of the minds of critical thinkers at the end of the 20th century. Indeed it flows from a variety of progressive traditions in social work and elsewhere that have challenged the status quo, questioned ourselves as professionals and made us look at the essential character of what we are doing with and to the people with whom we work. These traditions stretch back over the decades and the material you will see presented here owes much to the concepts and language of those who espoused: socialist practice, Marxist social work, radical social work, anti-racist social work, feminist practice and structural social work to name only a few.

There are a number of people who have been important to development and production of this monograph. Darlene Savoy and Sheila Oliver offered their technical, editorial and artistic talents to the design of the monograph. We also offer thanks to people who reminded us of important terms and offered us valuable definitional assistance: Jane Aronson, Professor, School of Social Work, McMaster University; Laurel Curley, MSW, Cayuga Nation; Jan Johnstone, MSW, activist; Anthony M. Hutchinson, activist; Kelly Garabto, blogger on environmental issues.

GLOSSARY OF TERMS FOR ANTI-OPPRESSIVE PERSPECTIVES ON POLICY AND PRACTICE*

The hope of remaking the world is indispensable in the struggle of oppressed men and women.
– Paulo Freire

Our Orientation

While it is probably quite obvious in the use of our own language, it may be important to point out that, in undertaking this project we, as editors and social work researchers, do so from a particular position. We are committed to what we believe is a well founded position, that social work operates in a world where inequality exists to a very significant degree. We take the position that social workers can take the side of the oppressed or the oppressor, that our work is never neutral. It is with this in mind that we have come to develop this glossary.

Why this Glossary?

The purpose of anti-oppressive practice in social work is, among other things, to assist people in unraveling the threads of multiple oppressions and the intersection and interaction among their various forms. In other words, we hope to be able to help people to identify how personal problems are developed and maintained through the interplay of public or structural issues. For example, child neglect or criminal behaviour can be seen to be rooted in conditions of poverty and discrimination. These, in turn, can be linked to the concentration of economic and political power. None of these relationships is simple and the way we investigate and express them is important. Not surprisingly, since social work is so heavily dependent on language communication, the words and terms we use with the people with whom we work as well as with each other and the general public are crucial. A great deal of the language that has been developed to enable us to discuss issues of subjugation, oppression and liberation is complicated. This should not surprise us given the complexities of the issues that they are meant to address. At the same time however, in the striving for novelty and precision, particularly in the academy, the language that has been developed is sometimes seen and experienced as difficult and inaccessible. It can appear alienating. There is clearly an irony in developing a language about oppression and liberation that ends up distancing academics from students and professionals from the people they are supposed to be assisting. For this reason we have put together this glossary of terms that tend to be utilized in discussions of the issues and practices that are the stuff of anti-oppressive social work. We hope that the material provided is meaningful and useful.

Layout of the Glossary

The terms are presented in alphabetical order and not organized around particular topics. Each of the definitions was constructed out of sources individually referenced, or developed by specific contributors listed on the inside back cover. We have also included quotes, usually from well-known activists and writers, which we hope will stimulate some thinking about the material.

---

* The original initiative and research for the project, of which this monograph is a part, was funded by the Faculty of Social Sciences Experiential Education Initiative and the Centre for Leadership in Learning, both at McMaster University.

Glossary

[T]hey came first for the Communists and I didn't speak up because I was not a Communist. Then they came for the trade unionists and I didn't speak up because I wasn't a trade unionist. Then they came for the Jews and I didn't speak up because I wasn't a Jew. Then they came for me and by that time no one was left to speak up.
- Martin Niemoeller, Minister

Ableism

The systematic oppression of people with disabilities. This form of oppression is manifest in the combination of personal prejudices, cultural expressions, and values, as well as social forces that marginalize people with disabilities and portray them in a negative light, thus oppressing them. The 'disability' itself has been socially constructed as a form of dependency in that disabled persons are regarded as helpless, dependent, needy, asexual, and unable to contribute to society. Resultantly, (similar to other forms of oppression) people with disabilities, who have little acknowledged value in a capitalist economy, are devalued and dehumanized. An important implication of the attitudes that people with disabilities must face is their marginalization and thus differential treatment at the hands of government. For example, while high income able bodied people are deemed worthy of tax breaks, people who have various forms of physical disabilities (themselves citizens and tax payers) must lobby hard merely to gain recognition for their right to equal access to buildings and public transportation. (Mullaly, 2002:167)

Aboriginal

Since contact in Canada, the original populations have been named and renamed a number of times by those other than themselves. Often times, those whose labels have been widely accepted were either confused or had ulterior motives and/or hidden agendas. In many cases, the oppressive historical context enforced acceptance of the labels by both the oppressed and the oppressor.

Aboriginal – refers to the residents of Canada who are biologically related to a group through bloodlines either maternally or paternally. Thus "aboriginal" encompasses those people who may be Native, First Nation, Indian, Status, Non-status, Metis and Inuit. The basic concept of aboriginality is most relevant to ancestry which relates to the first quadrant of the eastern teaching Medicine Wheel; that is, the physical reality of the individual.

First Nation – refers to the current legal term applied to Native people within the legislative and jurisdictional arenas of contemporary Canada. The phrase First Nation seems to be an active effort by the federal government to correct historical wrongs in terms of legislative terminology recognizing the chronological existence of peoples in Canada. The term also is used in various current agreements between Canada and her constructed and contested social concepts of aboriginal Nations; that is, through the legal reality of Band Councils as developed under the Indian Act in analyzing these constructed realities, one may find that Band Councils are quite dissimilar to the original Nations they have been designed to replace. The underlying difference relates most clearly to the difference between Indigenous and Indian; that is, the first is an authentic ancient reality while the second is an inauthentic contemporary construction.

Indian – refers to the past and current legal standing of aboriginal people under the Indian Act. This label was originally and inaccurately applied by a confused explorer upon his arrival in "the New World." It continues to be applied inaccurately as the defining legal term regarding roles and responsibilities between Canada and Native peoples as determined by the Indian Act. Other terms used under the Indian Act are "Status" and "Non-status" meaning those individuals who are recognized as Indians and those who are not. A Status Indian has greater accessibility to the benefits of the Act than a Non-status Indian does. An individual has "Status" when s/he meets the requirements of the Act to be legally recognized as an Indian; they are "Non-status" when, at some point, an event took place that interfered with the application of that legal term. For example, a Native woman who had Status, could lose her Status (and forfeit her children's and descendants' Status) through marriage to a non-Status man; a Status individual could choose to enfranchise – give up one's status as a "registered Indian" and thus all rights under the Indian Act (for example, if s/he wished to vote) or could be enfranchised by the government for various reasons; and, until recent times, a Status individual who joined the clergy, fought in a war or went to university could and usually did lose their Status. With each of these examples and others, the resulting situation was one of the person(s) involved becoming Non-status Indians.

Indigenous – refers to those individuals and groups who share and maintain the traditional cultural and spiritual understandings and world views of their ancestors. That is, "Indigenous" depicts those people who belong to the original understandings of various aboriginal groups; for example, Hodinoshonni (Iroquois), Denendeh (Dene), Anishnabec (Ojibway), and so on. The term "Indigenous" typically relates to the mentality and spirituality of those determined to maintain their original ways; that is, their ways of thinking and being members of the specific Nations into which they were born and to which they belong. Thus, the word "Indigenous" can be seen as directly corresponding to two quadrants of the Medicine Wheel; specifically, the mental and spiritual aspects of being.

Native – refers to those individuals and groups who see themselves or their existence as being directly or indirectly related to an indigenous or aboriginal reality. Thus, the term "Native" can be used for any context in which definitive terms are not required. Also, this word can be used correctly by anyone who may not be certain of the applicable conceptual boundaries of the Native individual or group to whom they refer. (Laurel Curley)

Acculturation

A term often used to refer to the psychological (i.e., behaviours, meaning-making) processes that people from two different cultural groups endure when coming into continuous first-hand contact. While some specific patterns may be altered, each group remains distinct. Although this is supposed to be a two-way process, members of minority groups rather than members of the dominant society make most of the changes. For the most part, this process of learning is imposed upon members of minority groups. There may be various pathways that may be "chosen." Some of these are: assimilation, marginalization, integration, segregation and biculturalism. Each will bring negative and positive outcomes for the people involved. Acculturation may take up to two or three generations. Thus for the people involved it may add another layer of stress and complexity regarding the individual's or the family's life cycle. In fact, one may say that acculturation is an added life stage for the people involved. (Mirna Carranza)

Activism

The belief, based on the position that the prospects of democracy are improved as people become engaged in using the process in their own interests and in solidarity with others. It suggests that individuals and groups have a right and a responsibility to organize and voice their concerns about issues concerning the public good. It rejects the notion that elites, politicians and experts should and can be left to make laws and policy without input from the public. (Borovoy, 1991:X)

Advocacy

The act of representing or defending others to gain or maintain the resources or rights that will allow for the meeting of a legitimate need which has been denied or threatened with removal. Advocacy is as old as society itself. There have always been significant differentials of power in society, and people have always needed and acquired assistance in dealing with more powerful people and institutions. In social work, it refers to championing the rights of individuals or communities through direct intervention or through empowerment. It is a basic obligation to the social work profession. Advocacy is not seen as a revolutionary endeavour, but focuses on improving inhumane or unfair conditions, primarily on a micro level. It may be said that advocacy is one end of a continuum that has, at the opposite end, large-scale social movement systems change. Most definitions of advocacy indicate the idea of conflict. (Barker, 1987: 4; Lee, 2001: 10-11)

Affinity Groups

Small groups of activists (usually from 3-20) based on a common ideology (e.g., environmental issues) or a shared concern for a given issue (e.g., peace or anti-globalization) or a common activity. They work together on direct action (see below). These groups are small enough to be able to be organized in a non-hierarchical manner, usually using consensus decision making, and are often made up of trusted friends or other like-minded people. Thus they provide a method of organization that can be spontaneous and tends to be responsive, flexible and decentralized. (Bill Lee)

Ageism

The oppression of a group of people solely on the basis of their age. Age is not only a process of biological maturation; it is also a social division wherein power, privilege and opportunities are allocated to some and withheld from others. The two main groups affected in a negative way are children and older people. Although some societies, such as traditional Aboriginal communities in North America, accord the elderly with power and respect, for the most part, older citizens are now associated with death, senility, madness and uselessness. Moreover, because the elderly are excluded from the labour force, they are no longer perceived to be making a contribution to the capitalist economy and hence they have little value as persons in a capitalist society. Similarly, children, while accorded a pseudo value in their role as potential consumers, remain unacknowledged as citizens. While family values are trumpeted, children are treated as property in cases of divorce and infrastructure that can nurture their development such as day care and education are under funded. (Mullaly, 2002: 166)

Agency

The faculty of or ability for acting or of exerting power. A person or group can be said to have or demonstrate agency when they utilize whatever form of power they possess to influence conditions or situations in which they find themselves. (Bill Lee)

Alienation .

A sense of social isolation or estrangement from our fellow human beings and a feeling that we are unable to influence them or events. It also can describe a sense of depersonalization, a belief that we (and others) do not matter. Writers like Weber saw alienation as a result of bureaucratic process (See Bureaucracy) while more recent thinkers like Freire and Fromm have pointed out that various forms of oppression lead to feelings of powerlessness and isolation. In a sense, it is the opposite of empowerment. (Bullock, 2002)

Analysis

A systematic consideration of any event, situation or process in terms of its respective parts. As well it involves thinking about the relationship between and/or among those parts, and the relationship of each part to the whole. For example as part of assisting with a problem that a family or a community might be experiencing, we would help the members examine the relationship among themselves, their networks and the various pressures exerted by the larger environments (social, economic and political) in which they live. (Barker, 1987)

Anarchism

Anarchism is simultaneously a political theory and a practice for life. As a theory, anarchism advocates for the creation of anarchy (see Anarchy below) to replace our current systems of oppression such as capitalism, colonialism, imperialism, and patriarchy. As a practice for life, anarchism outlines the ways in which we should organize ourselves, our workplaces, our communities, and our relationships so that they reflect, and enable us to work towards anarchy. Thus, anarchists intentionally work to remove all forms of authority and hierarchy, as well as instill democratic processes grounded in solidarity into all aspects of their lives. They envision this practice as the method through which people will develop the consciousness and skills necessary to both bring about revolution and to maintain an anarchist society thereafter. In other words, the means become the way to the end as principles of anarchy are used to organize the struggle for a new society. (Meghan Ross)

Anarchist

An anarchist is someone who adopts the theories of anarchism and works towards the development of anarchy – common ownership, self management, democratic planning led by the working class, and production for need rather than profit – (See Anarchism). Within anarchism, anarchists are differentiated according to the strategic approach they use to achieve anarchy, working as a 'mass anarchist/anarcha-communist' or an 'insurrectionary anarchist.' Both approaches are grounded in a shared history of anti-capitalism, anti-authoritarianism and opposition to hierarchy, and the struggle for freedom and liberty that is developed within the context of direct democracy and equality. They differ in that mass anarchists/anarcha-communists believe that only mass movements of people can create a revolutionary change in society. As such, they focus on participating in the struggles of working class people against the oppressions most directly impacting their lives, to win radical reforms building towards the revolution. Insurrectionists believe that any reforms gained are illusionary as those with privilege will develop new manifestations of oppression to accommodate change. They also believe that formal organizations are inherently authoritarian. As such, they emphasize participation in drastic deeds which capture people's attention enough to create revolutionary public upsurge. (Meghan Ross)

Anarchy

Anarchy is often mistakenly used to mean chaos or without order, and thus the misconception exists that those identifying as anarchists believe people should be able to do 'what they want whenever they want' without interference. The term is actually derived from the Greek word 'anarchos' meaning the "lack of ruler or authority." Thus, anarchists aim to create a society where individuals freely cooperate together as equals, with no rulers or authorities governing. Anarchists are not merely against authority because it is authority; they reject any social, economic, or political relationship that enables concentration of power and privileges some over others. (Meghan Ross)

Androcentrism

The term – its first use seems to have occurred in the early 20th century – indicates the tendency of society to value, emphasize or centre on the male and the male view of the world and everything in it. Thus, values and characteristics that are understood as centred on the female are judged (often negatively) in relation to a "male ideal." It is understood that this male centredness is common in a wide range of areas of life including history, religion, science, literature and art for example. A useful example of this androcentric idea is the term "history" which can be seen as a combination of "his" and "story" which implies that women do not have any past, at least not one worth mentioning. (Cecelia Lee)

Anthropocentrism

Linked to the notion of speciesism (Ryder, 2000), this is the belief that humans must be considered at the centre of, and have rights above any other aspect of reality, sentient or otherwise. This is a central concern for some environmentalists and animal rights activists. (McPherson, 2009)

Anti-Oppressive Practice (AOP)

A form of social work that focuses its intervention on social divisions and structural inequalities. AOP is concerned with themes of power, social justice, and inequality; and it values equality, freedom, both individuality and collectivity, and cooperation. The essence of AOP is based on the following: (1) acknowledgement of the effects of the structural dimensions of oppression which cut across class, gender, sexual orientation, ability, and so on; (2) adoption of self-reflective and critical stances on the part of workers; (3) promotion of co-participatory rather than authoritarian practice; and (4) commitment to working with and for the oppressed populations to achieve social transformation. AOP does not blame people, either individuals or groups, for the oppression they experience; it does not seek to assimilate oppressed groups into the mainstream, nor does it seek merely to compensate oppressed people with goods and services. AOP is a politically saturated practice that views itself through the constructive use of anger directed toward social injustice. (Wolfson, 2002: 18; Dominelli, 1996: 271, cited in Wolfson, 2002: 8; Mullaly, 2002: ix-x, 210)

> *You and I are close, we intertwine; you may stand on the other side of the hill once in a while, but you may also be me, while remaining what you are and what I am not.*
> **– Trinh T. Minh-ha**

Anti-Racism

Any work that aims to highlight and overturn the social and personal processes that maintain the power and privilege of one racial group over another. This can include teaching, working in practice or developing policies, as well as acting consciously in our day-to-day lives to confront and overcome racist laws, regulations, words, behaviours and attitudes. (Bill Lee)

Anti-Racism Organizational Change

Anti-racism organizational change aims to challenge systemically entrenched barriers in order to shift organizational cultures to become more inclusive. The goal of anti-racism organization change is to promote access, equity and full participation of those who do not come from the dominant culture group. This can be met with resistance as it interferes with the power relations and traditional privileges of members of the mainstream – e.g., white, male, Euro-North American – social groups. Such forthcoming changes are not restricted to the organizational culture, but are also linked to the system, policies, and practices of the organization. (June Ying Yee)

Anti-Racist

Anti-racist social workers hold the view that our laws, social institutions, and ideological climate favour white people as the dominant group over people of colour. For example, in North America and Europe, positions of privilege are enjoyed by white people, while people of colour experience social problems in greater numbers and with more severity. In other words, white people enjoy their privilege at the expense of people of colour by way of an oppressive system of social relations and an unjust set of social conditions. (Mullaly, 2002:15)

Anti-Semitism

Negative attitudes and discrimination on the basis of race and/or religion directed against Jews. The history of anti-Semitism is almost as old as Judaism itself, dating back to the 1st century BC.

Though very strong in various parts of Europe, particularly eastern Europe in the 18th and 19th centuries, in the 20th century, it reached its peak between 1941 and 1944 when six million Jews were systematically murdered or worked to death during the Holocaust. (Bullock, 1977: 39-40)

Assimilation

A term often used to describe a process that people go through either when they move to a new society (i.e., new immigrants or refugees) or are perceived as "different" (Aboriginal People) from the dominant society. Therefore, they are often expected to renounce significant aspects of their way of life. That is, cultural norms (e.g., specific clothing for men or women) and traditions, values, religious beliefs, language, etc. in order to be deemed acceptable by the society at large. This process is often "expected" or "chosen" by the people living at the margin of a specific society in order to belong, fit in, or be accepted. This process may be perceived as oppressive by those going through it – as there may be several negative consequences if they resist it. Some may become further marginalized or stigmatized if they do not conform to social expectations. The context of the specific society permeates this process (i.e., Canada's multicultural policy vs. the United States' assimilation policy). (Mirna Carranza)

Bureaucracy

An organizational form characterized by legal rules, a salaried administrative staff, the specialization of function, the authority of office, and the keeping of written records and documents. It is based on the belief that, more than any other form of social organization, it enables the precise calculation of the best means available to achieve a given end. Precision, speed, predictability, knowledge of files, continuity, discretion, unity, strict subordination, reduction of material and personal costs – these are the characteristics of a strictly bureaucratic organization. The great sociologist Max Weber identified two troublesome aspects of this development. First, modern bureaucracies are tremendously influential organizations composed of non elected officials. Consequently, they concentrate power and threaten democracy. Second, officeholders in bureaucratic organizations are not only discouraged from determining the goals of the organization, but are rather encouraged to think only of the best way to achieve those goals which are defined by their superiors. In this structure, workers are implicitly (and explicitly) expected to 'check their brains at the door.' It is also a form of organization that is deliberately rigid (to avoid undue personal influences) thus it can atrophy and become resistant to necessary adaptation and change. (Bullock, 1977: 98-99; Lee, 2011)

Capital

The term "capital" refers to wealth or assets. For Karl Marx capital in the industrial era is linked to one's relationship to the means of production; hence the term "capitalism" is used as a way of describing the current social order. In this order the bourgeoisie own the means of production (ownership of industries etc.) and the proletariat own only their labour power. Marx sees this system as unequal because the proletariat depend entirely on exchanging their labour power for wages provided by the bourgeoisie and lack the class consciousness or solidarity to see and act on the fact that the bourgeoisie also depend on their labour. Consequently the bourgeoisie maximize and build their capital by exploiting proletariat labour power (see class). The concept of capital, therefore, is inextricably linked to the issue of power within society. Other social scientists have more nuanced interpretations of capital than Marx. Pierre Bourdieu (1986), for instance, extends the notion to a broader sphere of exchange to recognize that class-based power (in the Marxist sense) of economic capital is at the root of all other types of capitals, but sees these as converting into symbolic forms that serve to give social inequality a natural and legitimate appearance. Cultural capital and social capital are the two major symbolic forms of capital. In Bourdieu's conception, capitals both structure the power positions of a field (see field) and in turn are products of a field, and as such capital is field-specific. (Winnie Lo)

Capitalism

Predominantly understood as an economic system composed of the following traits: 1) the continuous effort to expand wealth; 2) the co-ordination of a network of markets; and 3) a characteristically dual system of power, business enterprise and government. Under capitalism, workers are legally free to sell their labour to owners of capital, and owners of capital (a minority number of the populations) are legally free to invest their capital in order to maximize profits. Few analysts have thought of capitalism as a permanent system, but it has become unquestionably the most influential mode of economic organization in our time. (Brym, 1998: 27; Leckachman, 1981: 3-4; Bullock, 1977: 103)

Citizenship

Commonly refers to being a member of a nation, and the concomitant rights and obligations. In different eras, however, different classes and groups have gained enough power to change and expand citizenship rights as new classes and other groups have come onto the political stage. In the 18th century, the fight for civil citizenship occurred – the right to free speech, freedom of religion, and justice before the law. In the 19th and early 20th century, the fight for political citizenship occurred – the right to run for office and vote. Most of the 20th century was a struggle for social citizenship – the right to a certain level of economic security and full participation in the social life of the country. Finally, there continues to be a struggle for universal citizenship (see Social Citizenship) – the extension of rights to all adult members of society who have previously been excluded on the basis of gender, sexual orientation, race and/or ability. Some include the rights of humanity – the right to peace, security, and a clean environment – under universal citizenship. (Brym, 1998: 471-474)

Class

The position of an individual or a family within an economic hierarchy, along with others who have similar amounts of access to, or control over, material resources. (See Classism, Middle-Class) For example, members of the working class have incomes and influence significantly less than do members of the middle class and much less than members of the upper class. (Brym, 1998: 183)

Classism

Classism is not only a factor in inequalities of wealth, privilege, and power – it is both the result and the foundation of all other forms of oppression. Oppression such as sexism, racism and heterosexism help keep the hierarchy of power in place, while class is that hierarchy. Classism is the beginning point and the end product of all other forms of oppression. It is the essential structure of society, the sum total of all other inequalities. For example, we will find more people with disabilities the lower we look in the class strata. Therefore, class becomes the result of discrimination against people with disabilities. Similarly, oppression directed towards those in a lower class, or classism, further limits the quality of life of those same people with disabilities because they have less access to the wealth and power required to remove oppressive barriers in society. (Bishop, 2002b: 83; Bishop, 2002a: 46)

Collective Trauma

This is a relatively new concept in social science. While in general terms it can refer to the impact on groups of any disaster of natural or human causation, in anti-oppressive social work it typically focuses on the manner in which, specifically, human-made events designed to force people from specific groups into a "desired" way of life have impacted its members. For the most part, collective trauma is the result of some form of violence and oppression toward individuals with the intent to disperse the collective functioning of entire communities. Examples of this can be found all through history (e.g., colonization and so-called ethnic cleansing). More specifically, the injury of trauma hinders group members in joining in solidarity in order to resist oppressive circumstances. The long-lasting effects of collective trauma may be that the group member's ability to work together and to live in harmony, with the intent to look after the welfare and survival of each other for the benefit of the entire community is effected. The effects may present themselves in subtle ways; i.e., mistrust among community members, severe alcohol use among a significant percentage of members of a specific group. At times, collective trauma influences group identity and segregates members of the affected community to live with shame and/or at the margin of a specific society. (Mirna E. Carranza)

Colonialism

This process has two foci. The first is economic where the colonizer group appropriates the resources of the subject people for their specific material benefit. Second, and as part of the first focus, it seeks to maintain a sharp distinction between the ruling power and the colonial (exploited) populations. Unequal rights are a fundamental feature of colonialism, as is the imposition of a dominant culture's values and practices on that of a subordinate group. This imposition of values and practices is usually accompanied by a rhetoric of providing "help," "democracy," "civility," "economic development" and/or "salvation." (See Imperialism) (Bullock, 1977: 418-19; Lee, 1992)

Communism

Historically, the point of reference for communism is the principle of collective ownership of all property. Modern communism is linked with the ideas of Karl Marx and the concept of a classless society based on the notion of collective ownership of the means of production. Communism can be understood as an ideology that preserves capitalism's inventiveness, but puts it directly to human uses rather than allowing it to be channelled through the market for the purpose of maximizing profits. It is to be a society without a state, and without coercive institutions. Ideally, everyone cooperates for the common good. There will be no limits to the development of individual human potential as all are free to develop a wide range of talents and interests. (Bullock, 1977:143; Garner, 1996:159)

Educate, Organize, Resist!
– Bumper Sticker

Community Organizing

This term which has been used alternatively to the somewhat problematic term community development (See Development) has a significant history. It was first utilized to denote how community agencies come together to address social issues. Later, in the 1960s the term became identified with the confrontational approach of Saul Alinsky (1971) which saw grass roots groups, usually based in neighbourhoods, take on power holders. More recently it has been embraced somewhat more broadly as a social intervention which seeks to maximize the ability of oppressed or disadvantaged people to take action and influence their environments. It goes about this task by facilitating a growing understanding of their social, political and economic environments and of themselves as citizens. The aim is to develop power so that they are able to act: to acquire resources; change inadequate institutions and laws; or build new ones, more responsive to their needs and those of all human beings. (Lee, 2011)

Conjunctural Analysis

Refers to the systematic and rigorous consideration of an immediate situation focusing on the examination of the balance of personal, social, economic and political forces at a given moment (or conjuncture) and the opportunities for action short or long term. It is founded on the notion that, for example, a community or social movement organization, in developing an action plan to challenge a situation of economic or racial discrimination, would look at the various elites and civil society groups, attitudes in the general population, and recent significant events in order to decide how to frame an issue and begin a campaign. For example, in a conjunctural analysis we would want to consider the personality traits of key leaders as well as the interests of particular institutions. (Naming the Moment Project; Whitmore and Wilson, 1997: 59)

Conscientization

Refers to the phenomenon that exists in and for the struggle for liberation from oppression. It is a process that enables individuals to view themselves not as objects to be exploited, controlled or oppressed. Rather, it allows individuals to recognize themselves as subjects with dignity and worth, which should not be conditional upon race, gender, class or any other inherent characteristics. This concept was developed by Paulo Freire in the 1960s as an instrument for the transformation of the social order. It is seen as emerging out of praxis – a practice in which theory and action are dialectically related to one another (meaning that each is analytically testing the truth of the other). (See Praxis) (Bullock, 1977: 159; Freire, 2000; Wolfson, 2002: 22)

Conservatism

Refers to a doctrine of enthusiasm for capitalism (and the free market economy) combined with support for patriotism of the electorate, an emphasis on social order, and moral discipline based on traditional values that are seen to have withstood the test of time. It seeks to preserve the authority of the state, but limits it to national defense and overseeing the marketplace. It also seeks to strengthen institutions such as the family, schools, and churches as tools of securing sound morality. (Bullock: 162)

Constructivism and Constructionism

Constructivism refers to a broad range of conceptual approaches that consider "truth" to be constituted from individual subjectivity and social interaction. In other words, constructivism contends that truth is not out there in the world waiting to be discovered, but is constructed by people. The construction of "truth" in a person's mind or within society by groups of social actors represent the two major foci of constructivism. Although the overarching term constructivism tends to be used to refer to both these foci, the term constructivism refers to a focus on internal cognitive schemas, while the term constructionism refers to a focus on social variables. Within this delineation, an example of "constructivist" thought is Piagetian psychology where the ability to make sense of the world is both enabled and constrained by the cognitive schema (ways of thinking) of the knower. An example of "constructionism" is the ways society as a whole makes sense of and constructs events and knowledge. It is important not to place too much emphasis on the distinction between constructivism and constructionism because the similarities between them are greater than their differences. The closer one examines these approaches the more the distinctions between them begin to blur – Piaget, for instance, argued that one cannot neatly separate the biological, psychological, and social. Perhaps this blurring explains why, despite attempts to distinguish between constructivists and constructionists, social work literature tends to use the terms interchangeably. (Gary C. Dumbrill)

Critical

A stance that points us toward seeking underlying causes and effects that are not clearly seen in everyday discourse. For example, a capitalist society formally views the market as 'free,' the bureaucracy as 'rational,' and the political system as 'democratic;' however, in no case do any of these institutions truly live up to the promise of their formal principles. For example, markets, rather than being free, are dominated by huge corporations, bureaucratic processes become rigid and obstruct creativity, while the political system is dominated by wealthy elites. (Bullock, 1977: 185)

Critical investigation helps people to look at social problems in the light of what they wish to achieve as self-reliant and self-determining social beings.
– Susan McGrath, Activist and Teacher

Critical Analysis

This approach to knowledge development uses the principles of critical thinking (see Critical Thinking below) to explore the assumptions, values and knowledge bases underpinning established social work theories and practices. Through questioning, one seeks to expose the processes of domination replicated through social work practices. Critical analysis requires that the social worker be aware of one's own worldview and social location. Critical analysis leads to both understanding and transformative practice. (Sheila Sammon)

Critical Consciousness

The understanding of how personal worlds are organized and constrained by power structures and assumptions not readily visible in our everyday lives, then asking how that happens and how the injustices and inequalities that result might be changed. (See Critical Thinking) (Jane Aronson)

Critical Disability Theory

This theory is associated with the Critical Medical model of Anthropology, the social Model of Disability and the Rights Outcome approach to disability and focuses on three principles or themes. First, it seeks to explain that the manner in which disability is perceived and diagnosed scientifically and socially frames the manner in which people with disabilities are treated as a collectivity (Roeher Institute, 1996). Second and aligned to this is that the notion of disability must be deconstructed so that it not seen as an individual issue but one to be addressed as a consequence of structural inequality. Third, policy analysts and activists must look to the disabled to define their challenges and to provide leadership in finding solutions. (Katherine Schliecher, Vanessa Rankin & Michelle Gibson)

Critical Theory

Refers to the development of criticisms and alternatives to traditional or mainstream social theory. Critical theory is motivated by an interest in those who are oppressed, is informed by a critique of domination, and is driven by a goal of liberation. Its commitment is to changing the world in ways that can help emancipate those on the margins of society. It opposes positivism, engages in consciousness-raising, views oppression in structural terms, and endorses the notion of people being responsible for their own liberation. The following are 3 undertakings of critical theory: (1) locate the sources of domination in social practices; (2) present an alternative vision of a life free from such domination; and (3) translate, if necessary, to ensure that such a vision is understood by those who are oppressed in society. (Mullaly, 2002: 15-17)

What has to be explained is not the fact that the [person] who is hungry steals or the fact that the [person] who is exploited strikes, but why the majority who are hungry don't steal and why the majority of those who are exploited don't strike.
– Wilhelm Reich

Critical Thinking

A process of looking beyond surface appearances to understand how personal worlds are organized and constrained by power structures and assumptions not readily visible in our everyday lives … asking how that happens and how the injustices and inequalities that result might be changed. (Jane Aronson)

Culture

Patterns of beliefs, symbols and values that develop over time among groups of people. It is the symbolic order through which people communicate and organize their social life. Culture helps people adapt to their environment and it usually facilitates group survival. It provides both a glue that binds us together, and a boundary that identifies our differences from others. Culture is a much broader term than ethnicity. It revolves around the fact that groups differ in their worldview, their perspectives on patterns of life, their concept of the essential nature of the human condition, and the way they structure behaviour. It is influenced by many factors including one's social location, language, family and social relationships. Culture often runs so deep that one may be unconscious of its influence, and hence misinterpret it as an objective reality. (See Ethnicity, Social Location) (Wong, 2002: 32; Brym, 1998: 27, 71; Lee, 2011, Glossary)

Cultural Competence

This term is sometimes regarded as synonymous with "cultural sensitivity," yet it has a different meaning. Similar to cultural sensitivity the term refers to an ability to work and communicate across cultural difference, but it conceptualizes this skill as emerging from: an awareness of one's own culture, biases, beliefs and prejudices; an awareness of and openness to cultures, values and ways of being different to one's own; and an understanding of how the power of racism and other forms of oppression shape the way culture and difference are socially constructed. Although this definition of cultural competence is quite compatible with anti-oppressive practice, because the term is often used as if synonymous with "cultural sensitivity," one should check the way it is being used before assuming that it is being used in an anti-oppressive manner. (Gary Dumbrill)

Cultural Genocide

A pattern of intentional acts, including laws and regulations, developed by the state and its institutions in order to undermine and eradicate the cultural legacies and/or practices of specific groups of people. More often than not, these traditional practices are perceived as having the potential to erode and/or threaten the standards of the groups in power. As a result these cultural and/or traditional practices are forced to the margins of society and in extreme cases (for example, various Aboriginal practices like the Potlatch and Longhouse ceremonies were prohibited by the government of Canada) they go underground and are carried out in secret and as a form of resistance to the state as well as for their own sake. (Mirna E. Carranza)

Cultural Imperialism

The replacement of a traditional culture by the imported culture of a dominant group or society that controls the means of communication. For example, the power of large American television and publishing corporations has saturated many countries with American culture. Another example would be First Nations people in Canada who were not always given a choice about the introduction of TV into their communities despite their expressed concerns. (Brym, 1998: 58)

Cultural Sensitivity

To be culturally sensitive is to be aware of the way that culture can shape perception and meaning when interacting with others. The term is often used in international business communications, but when used in social work refers to a worker being sensitive to such issues when intervening across cultural difference. The term is problematic from an anti-oppressive perspective when it leads to one assuming that the knower is from the dominant social group, that this group is culturally neutral, and that the person to be known is invariably culturally different. Such thinking sets the dominant group as the unexamined and taken-for-granted societal norm, and constructs the "other" as an outsider who needs special sensitivity to be understood. Despite these problems with the term, the concept is sound if one accepts that we all exist in many cultural contexts and that we need to be aware of how this impacts communication and meaning between all individuals in society. The concept is also problematic when attempting to operationalize it in a social work setting. It implies that the social worker must understand all clients' cultures. This is not only impossible but leads to stereotyping and classifying behaviours. (Gary Dumbrill & Sheila Sammon)

Deconstructivism

This term refers to the interpretive techniques used to unpack a discourse and bring its hidden assumptions and arguments to light. By understanding discourses as contested sites of power and conflict, one can make better sense of the covert, almost invisible nature of ideology today. In this way, we can then make more sense of the dominant culture's current hegemony, while articulating a counter-discourse that points the way towards more egalitarian social relations, practices, and processes. For example, feminism has powerfully deconstructed the dominant patriarchal discourse, and developed a counter-discourse. (See Hegemony, Dominant Ideology) (Mullaly, 2002: 92)

To doubt everything or believe everything are two equally convenient solutions;
both dispense with the necessity of reflection.
– Jules Poincare (1854-1912)

Democracy

Broadly speaking, democracy means rule by the body of citizens and the right of all to decide what are matters of general concern. It is based on a belief in the value of the individual human being, and it exists to the extent that certain basic rights are guaranteed to every citizen. These rights are: 1) security against arbitrary arrest and imprisonment; 2) freedom of speech; 3) freedom of the press; 4) freedom of assembly (to hold public meetings); 5) freedom of petition and association (to form parties, and trade unions etc.); 6) freedom of movement; and 7) freedom of religion. Furthermore, democracy is required to have an established independent judiciary and courts to which all have access. Democracy has typically been exercised indirectly through the free election of representatives – representative democracy. (See Representative Democracy) (Bullock, 1977: 208-209)

Development

For many people (and institutions) this term is linked to notions of economic productivity and prosperity, eradicating poverty, and delivering democracy. Implicit within the word 'development' is the suggestion of change, of someone or something evolving, growing, maturing and progressing. In its pure form, development is an incremental process of reaching full potential. Pieterse notes that it can also be thought of as an organized involvement in the affairs of a community according to a standard of improvement. Clearly development is not a neutral term. Communities, countries, and continents are deemed 'developing,' 'developed,' 'maldeveloped' or 'un(der)developed,' suggesting perceptions of defined geographical areas achieving differing levels of economic, social, and political power and success. Development projects and aid, typically conceptualized, supported, and initiated by the global north and delivered in the global south, are generally understood to be about 'under-developed' communities and regions becoming 'developed,' or catching up to 'developed' countries. For some theorists like Kaplan the development era has been destroyed in the face of delusion, disappointment, and failure. Others however are not yet prepared to write its obituary. They believe that in its deconstruction, development can be reconstructed. Theorists like Pieterse offer a view of development as a field in flux, one that is defined by crisis, and characterized by processes and perspectives, which are dynamic and changing. Development, he suggests, is spearheaded by energetic questioning, critiquing and probing alternatives. For a practitioner like Kaplan, it is about the facilitation of a growing awareness and consciousness such that people are able to take control of their own lives and circumstances, and exert responsibility and purpose with respect to their future. He believes it to be an art in which people facilitate the growing consciousness of others, all the while demanding a critical awareness of their own self-development. (Janet Fishlock)

Dialectic

This term can have two meanings, which are related but not identical. First, the philosopher Hegel suggested it as a way of arriving at a truth. An argument is put forward (a thesis), then a counter argument is put forward (an antithesis); then, in a process that combines the two (synthesis) and resolves the original statements; finally a new "truth" is articulated. The second way of understanding the term is in the Marxian sense whereby a dominant system of thought or power, based on control of the material means of production, is contradicted by another. The resulting historical conflict process develops a new dominant system which in turn will be challenged by another. Marx saw this as the way history unfolds. (Bill Lee)

Dialogue

An exchange of knowledge and a process of co-learning which assumes an intrinsic equality between and among the people involved. Rooted in the approach of popular education, this is an important concept in anti-oppressive practice in that a commitment to dialogue undercuts the notion of social worker as powerful active expert and clientele as powerless, passive and uncomprehending of his/her own lives. (See Popular Education) (New Internationalist, 2003: 19)

Diaspora

Diaspora is often associated with Jewish migration. Since the nineteenth century, the term has become widely applied to the dispersal of the Jews throughout the Gentile nations and to the Jewish community that lives outside the frontiers of the biblical Israel. It is now also used to refer to the experience of populations displaced by slavery, colonialism or forced migration, as well as those individuals/groups that choose migration. It is also commonly used to describe history and experience of individuals living outside of their nation-state, as well as an imagined place. Therefore, those individuals who may have been in this nation-state may have 'diasporic feelings and thoughts' about a place of their ancestors. (Jan Jonstone)

Direct Action

This term suggests a method or theory (violent or nonviolent though often the latter) that seeks immediate remedies for perceived ills, as opposed to *indirect* tactics such as electing representatives who promise to provide remedy at some later date. Proponents of direct action view reformist politics as ineffective in bringing about change, providing participants with the illusion of success. This allows elites (political and/or economic) to maintain the basic set of power relations that underpins fundamental social problems. Direct action is seen as rendering the particular business or government institution incapable of operating effectively. Examples of direct action would include: strikes, protest marches, boycotts and blockades. (Lee, 2011; Tracy, 1996)

Discourse

A set of topics for discussion and a way of talking about those topics that is continued over time by a number of participants. Discourse includes not only language, but also the rules governing the choice and use of language and how the ideas and language will be framed. A discourse is a framework of thought, meaning and action, which does not reflect knowledge, reality, or truth, but creates and maintains them. Knowledge is produced by discourse – it is the way in which power, language and institutional practices combine to produce particular ways of thinking. Although there is always more than one discourse at any point in time, there is usually one dominant discourse. The current dominant discourse consists of a set of assumptions about the social world that largely reflects the interests of capitalism, patriarchy, and people of European descent. The concept of discourse is an important tool for understanding oppression and for developing anti-oppressive practices. (Mullaly, 2002: 22- 23) (Brym, 1998: 71)

Discourse Analysis

The analysis of a piece of text in order to reveal either the discourse operating within it or the linguistic and rhetorical devices that are used in its construction. (See Discourse) (Burr, 1995:184)

Discrimination

Unfair or unequal treatment of individuals or groups; prejudicial behaviour acting against the interests of those people who characteristically tend to belong to less powerful groups within society (women, disabled, people of colour, for example). Discriminatory practices deny individuals equal access to societal rewards. Discrimination is a matter of social formation as well as individual/group behaviour that stems from socialization. (Wolfson, 2002: 19; Brym, 1998: 221)

Diversity

In everyday usage, this term refers to characteristics of individuals such as race, culture, gender and sexual orientation. In social policy, the term relates to the reality that people in Canada occupy a different status and social location in relation to the state and its policies. (Graham, 2000: 63)

Dominance

Refers to ascendancy or taking precedence based on some form of power, or the behaviour pattern by which individuals establish the hierarchy of the group. The maintenance of dominance requires both aggression and submission. (See Power) (Fairchild, 1970: 98; Bullock, 1977: 235)

Dominant Ideology

Refers to the interests, perspectives, viewpoints, and understandings of the dominant class and other powerful groups. The ideology maintains the power and interests of this class. For example, the dominant class has control of the media, which tends to distribute its ideas, beliefs, values and norms thus creating acceptance and legitimization of the status quo. Ideologies based on collectivism and equality are subordinate to capitalist ideology, which is based on individualism and inequality. The dominant ideology is so ingrained that any other ideology or worldview is seldom given credence as a workable social or economic system. The existing systems are seen to be natural, normal, and inevitable. An analysis of the dominant ideology enables us to identify and expose those thought structures that rationalize oppression and, conversely, to promote countervailing ideologies based on social justice and equality. It also helps us to better understand 'internalized oppression,' which is why people will often develop loyalty to and defend a social system that discriminates against them. (See Status Quo, Internalized Oppression, Ideology, Capitalism) (Brym, 1998: 106; Bullock, 1977: 24)

> *The ruling ideas of each age have ever been the ideas of its ruling class.*
> – Karl Marx (1818-1883)

Efficacy

A term that suggests the ability of someone or something to achieve a desired end. In terms of human activity it has three important and interrelated components. First, it refers to a person's or group's ability to carry out an action. Second, it refers to a person's or group's sense or belief in its ability to produce desired results by their actions. Third, it suggests that the person or group has good reason to believe that the environment in which it is operating is amenable to productive action. (Bill Lee)

Elites

A privileged minority who have more power than the majority, and who use it, sometimes obviously (for example when police are used to hamper a union picket or a civil protest); sometimes covertly (for example through shaping the presentation of social issues in the media; or monitoring private telephone communication without seeking a court order) to support their advantaged position. (Lee, 2011, Glossary)

Empowerment

Gaining or regaining the capacity to interact with and/or change the environment in ways that enhance one's resources to meet our own needs, contribute to our well-being and potential, find satisfaction, and have as much control over our lives as possible. Empowerment also includes the development of a critical consciousness about the causes of injustice and powerlessness. Oppressive and discriminatory forces alienate people and erode their strengths; therefore, the social work role in the empowerment process is to help individuals develop their capacity to change their situation in order to ensure a better fit between their environment and their needs. (Lee, 2011; Hepworth et al, 2002: 438)

Environmental Racism

The term "environmental racism" emerged in the United States in the 1980s, but is now used across local, national and global contexts to reference a variety of concerns and questions about the ways in which environmental policies, planning and activism, expressions of environmentalism, and constructions of nature and the environment are informed by ideas about 'race,' and work to maintain and/or produce racism. While the term was used to describe the location of hazardous waste sites and polluting industries (as well as areas which are particularly threatened by the effects of climate change) in areas inhabited mainly by non-white and low-income peoples, the term also calls attention to ways in which notions of "the environment" are established through and work to reinforce dominant assumptions about "race," with gender, class, ability and sexuality, and to the operation of racism in environmental movements. This development compels interrogation of both issues of distribution and equality, and of the very way in which nature is imagined and governed, and environmental knowledge is produced. (Andil Gosine)

Epistemic Privilege

'Epistemology' means 'theory of knowledge.' The term 'epistemic privilege' links privileged or special knowing to social location. Epistemic privilege is the idea that people who are subordinated in particular power relations tend to know more about those power relations than people who are advantaged by them. So, for example, in general, men's knowledge about domestic work, and about sexual violence, tends to be distorted; women's knowledge of sexist relations is more accurate than men's. (Christina Sinding)

Essentialism

This is the belief that things and people have an inherent nature that defines them across space and time. Central to this notion is the idea that the nature of things can be uncovered and *known* once and for all. An example of essentialist thinking is the belief that we can find out the inherent nature of a group and we can use that to define everyone within the group across time and space. Today, most philosophers believe that the definitions we give things and people are influenced by our values and beliefs. While essentialism has been largely discredited as social science, it still operates in the hard sciences and in people's "common sense" thinking. (Sarah Todd)

Ethnicity

Ethnicity is a group membership in which the defining features are the characteristics of shared unique cultural traditions and a heritage that spans generations. It implies a shared past. It is a group with a sense of identity among members and with common geographical, religious, racial and cultural roots. At times, the term 'ethnic' has been used to imply race, but it is not synonymous. (See Race) (Wong, 2003: 31)

Ethnocentric Multiculturalism

A term that attempts to articulate the contradictory nature of Canadian multiculturalism. Canada's policy of multiculturalism gives the cultures of all Canadians a place in the nation, yet despite this policy the nation's norms, traditions and holidays are based on Western European (particularly English and to a lesser extent French) culture. Consequently, despite a policy of multiculturalism, Western European culture predominates as a form of ethnocentrism in Canada and it is only on the fringes of the nation that "other" cultures are accepted or "tolerated." This acceptance often takes the form of celebrating "diverse" cultures in food or dance festivals. Although this seems benevolent it occurs in the context of Western European culture, the unspoken dominant "norm" from which "difference" or "diversity" is measured. (Gary C. Dumbrill and Sarah Maiter)

Ethnocentrism

Refers to seeing the world from the point of view of only one ethnic tradition, while the perspectives of other ethnic groups are perceived as misleading or less useful. Members of European cultural groups have suggested that various indigenous cultures (for example in Australia and North America) are not as strong ethically or technically as their own. (Brym, 1998: 61)

Ethnostress

Refers to the situation that occurs when the sense of place in the world – cultural beliefs and/or positive identity – of a people is disrupted by their being relegated to the margins of society. An internal stress can arise when groups (for example, aboriginal peoples or gays and lesbians) must struggle to come to terms with the negative experiences they have as they interact with the dominant society. In essence, they are prevented from seeing themselves in a positive light. (Antone, Miller & Myers, 1986: 7)

False Consciousness

Refers to a form of internalized oppression. It occurs when groups of people hold false beliefs that are contrary to their own interest and that contribute to their disadvantaged position. A false consciousness views the world as given, as truth, and not as shaped through human action. Marx used the term to explain why the masses would accept capitalism when it was clearly exploitative. An individual not only sees herself through the eyes of the dominant group and judges herself on its values; but she also adopts them as her own, even at her own expense. For example, a person may escape from their gay identity and enter into a heterosexual union to ease the burden of their (internal and external) oppression. (See Internal Oppression) (Mullaly, 2002: 67 &129)

Fascism

Various Fascist movements reflect the very different national backgrounds of the countries in which they developed – the most famous historical examples are the Fascist Movement formed in 1919 which led Mussolini to power in Italy from 1922-1945 and the German Nazi movement under Hitler. There are contemporary examples such as Chile under Augusto Pinochet and even elements of the American administration under George Bush Jr. They all possess a few similarities. All are strongly nationalist, and violently anti-communist; all stand in opposition to liberalism, democracy and parliamentary parties; each seeks to impose an authoritarian state composed of one party, which has a monopoly of power; and, each is led by a single leader with charismatic qualities and dictatorial powers. Fascism was discredited by the defeat of the Fascist states in WWII. (Kershaw, 1998; Bullock, 1977)

Feminism

Refers to advocacy for the rights of women and is linked to a social movement for change. The feminist movement has never been a single, unified movement, and consequently, there is no single accepted definition of feminism. All feminists believe in equal rights and opportunities for women. Feminism emerged from a growing recognition that women were subordinated, discriminated against, and treated unequally on the basis of their sex. Feminism is, therefore, concerned with analyzing the domination of men over women in the household, in the paid labour force, and in the realms of politics, law and culture. Within the broad parameters of commonality, there are extensive differences: in political strategy, in visions about what constitutes women's liberation, in attitudes to men, in understanding the roots of women's oppression, in setting priorities, in identifying constituencies and allies. (Brym, 1998: 19; Bullock, 1997:314-315; Adamson et. al, 1988: 9)

> *The personal is political, in the kitchen as well as in the community.*
> **– Wendy Weeks, Feminist, activist, teacher**

Field

In Bourdieu's (1986) theory, a field can be thought of as a microcosm of larger society. There are a variety of these microcosms or fields – the discipline of social work, arts, and media are all examples of fields. A field is often compared to a game with governing rules, and each field is characterized by distinct set of capitals (see capital). People in a field compete for the accumulation of capitals, because capital is the currency to play the game. But the ultimate prize people compete for is the power to shape the field, which is the say to define the rules and capitals that favour them the most (see symbolic power and symbolic struggle). For instance in the field of social work, people with differing ideologies primarily compete to gain the capitals that define good practice and research, but the ultimate competition is to define the types of practice and research the profession should engage in. People in a field, therefore, have certain influence in shaping a field (e.g. setting the rules and determining what capitals are valued), despite the influence of external society. Simply put, a field is a site where people compete for the same stake. (Winnie Lo)

Free Market

A market that is not impeded by any form of government intervention. It is often referred to as 'laissez-faire,' let things be, no interference. The free market entails competition among individuals, companies and countries for scarce resources. Supporters of the free market ideology propose that unregulated markets and market activity will produce wealth and jobs that will trickle down to the poor. However, there is little evidence that indicates its success in this regard. Similarly, supporters argue that effort and skill will be rewarded in the free-market, while critics note that luck and status (often based on race, class, and sex) are equally or more likely to be rewarded. (Brym, 1998: 63 & 182; Bullock, 1977: 336; Lekachman, 1981: 149)

Genocide

A term coined by Lemkin referring to deliberate and planned acts which are aimed at eradicating, in whole or in part, any national, ethnic, racial or religious group. The attempted extermination of European Jewry by Fascists before and during WWII is a prime example, though there have been numerous examples:

Armenians by Turkey in 1915; Aboriginal people in North America, particularly in the U.S.A.; and in Rwanda, the Tutsis population by members of the Hutu people. (U.N. Convention on the Prevention and Punishment of the Crime of Genocide (CPPCG) article 2; Lemkin, 1944).

Globalization

Refers to the process of world social transformation that leaves no society untouched. Some have referred to it as the process that makes the world a single place, or that binds the population of the world into a single society. In this process, information, commodities and images (produced in a particular region of the world) enter into a global flow. Optimistic views suggest that globalization highlights the cultural diversity of nations; while others argue that globalization decreases the cultural differences between nations as all are subsumed into a single global culture, and that it is driven by cultural imperialism as it is Western goods, commodities, and information that dominate the flow. Critics have noted that globalization reaches into every aspect of life, transforming every activity and natural resource into a measured and owned commodity. It is about feeding the market's insatiable need for growth by redefining as 'products' entire sectors that were previously considered part of the public sphere and not for sale. The invading of the public by the private has reached into categories such as health and education, of course, but also into ideas, genes and even seeds and water. International trade law must be understood not only as taking down selective barriers to trade, but more accurately as a process that systematically puts up new barriers around knowledge, technology, and newly privatized resources. (Brym, 1998: 413; Bullock, 1977: 367; Klein, 2002:. xx-xxi)

> *As I have already said, the belief that one's own view of reality is the only reality is the most dangerous of all delusions. It becomes still more dangerous if it is coupled with the missionary zeal to enlighten the rest of the world, whether the rest of the world wishes to be enlightened or not.*
> **– Paul Watzlawick**

Habitus (from Bourdieu's theory)

Habitus is a structure that is responsible for our thoughts and actions. It is often understood as the embodiment of external social structure. However, Bourdieu (1986) constructs habitus in such a way to show that action is not determined purely by external social forces, nor by free will alone, but by a complex interplay between the two. Habitus, therefore, is conditioned but not determined by external social forces. The Latin term habitus denotes the idea that people usually act not out of conscious calculation, but out of unthought learned ways of thinking, feeling and acting, like a mental habit. Habitus has important implication in the reproduction, particularly the unconscious reproduction, of social differences and social inequalities. (Winnie Lo)

Hegemony

Refers to the ideological domination of one class by another. The most influential ideas are the ones that benefit the wealthiest economic class as the ruling class is generally successful in making its ideas appear to be the only plausible ideas. Often, ideological domination is attained through control over the media and other cultural institutions to represent the interests, values, and understandings of the capitalist class and other powerful groups as natural and universal. For example, the notions that 'cream rises to the top,' and the attainability of 'the American dream' are accepted as universal axioms, but rather are hegemonic and benefit powerful groups most. (Brym, 1998: 64, 71 &106)

Heterosexism

Institutions and values that promote heterosexuality as the superior (or only acceptable) form of sexuality, and one that is more natural. It oppresses gay, lesbian, and bisexual people, and arguably anyone that does not fit into the traditional one-man, one-woman monogamous relationship. One of the unique aspects of oppression towards homosexuality is its general lack of visibility. This is an impediment to organizing as a group since it is not known what the size of the group is and members are not known to one another. (Mullaly, 2002:165)

Historical Trauma

This is a term originally coined by Maria Brave-Heart-Jordan. It is the result of multiple and compounded layers of pain, grief and loss experienced over generations and contributing to underlying psychological wounding in individuals and groups. The wounding is understood as being passed on from one generation to the next without opportunity for processing and healing. Symptoms may include prolonged signs of acute grief, depression, substance abuse, etc. The concept is often applied to the situation of North American Aboriginal people who shortly after contact and throughout the generations have experienced acts of forced removal, killings, attempted assimilation and apartheid through the Indian Act. These originated in history but their effects are maintained and the underlying issues have not been addressed or redressed. It can apply equally to individuals or groups of people whose experience of loss has originated in prior generations, for example, the children of Jewish victims of Nazi genocide, Palestinian victims of forced removal from their homelands and where redress and/or healing is not complete. (Bonnie Freeman)

Homophobia

Refers to an irrational fear or hatred of or discomfort with homosexual people or homosexuality (including lesbian, transgendered and transsexual people) that is often manifest in individual violence or structural discrimination. (Mullaly, 2002:165)

Identity .

Refers traditionally to the relatively stable and enduring sense that a person has of oneself. One's identity is seldom, if ever, determined solely by one characteristic, although one or a few characteristics may be major markers of an individual, or be more prominent in more situations or contexts than others. These characteristics often include one's gender, sexual orientation, ethnicity and class. In developing our identities, we draw on culturally available resources, and on society as a whole, which is why an individual may find difficulties describing the source and nature of her various identities. (Bullock, 1977: 413; Mullaly, 2002:146)

Ideology

Any system of ideas that describes and explains the experiences of certain individuals and either justifies their situation or proposes alternatives to it. Ideologies provide frameworks for making sense of the social world; in other words, they provide us with a worldview. They may be the product of, for example, a set of values, experiences, and political beliefs. Often, our ideology is implicit and unstated (and usually culturally framed), though it is impossible to be without one. An ideology will determine the nature and casual explanations given to social problems, as well as the solutions to these problems, including the types of interventions and social work activities to be used. Ideology is the power of ideas that sustains or confronts discrimination, oppression and inequality. One of the most powerful ideologies in the world today is that of the free market economy. (See Free Market, Dominant Ideology) (Barker, 1987: 75; Brym, 1998: 61; Lee, 2011, glossary; Mullaly, 2002, 23)

Imperialism

A process by which a state extends its power. This is accomplished by acquiring territories (usually by conquest), forcibly imposing a system of government, and economically exploiting the inhabitants. (Bullock, 1977: 418)

Indigegogy

This is an evolving Indigenous education model, rooted in the worldview and traditions of Indigenous people, encompassing a processes and content of education which are wholistic - i.e., reflect and affect the mental-spiritual-physical-emotional aspects of the world and of those involved in the education process. It is a means of transferring knowledge that is built upon the inherent capacity of the learner to understand and to be valued. Teacher and learner are understood to be of equal value in the educational process and it is expected that the learner will know as much as the teacher at the end. An important principle is that the knowledge transferred becomes the responsibility of the learner and with the relationship that emerges between teacher and learner they will help each other to continue to carry the knowledge. The content being multifaceted, it can be empirically based but can also include the capacity to understand our relationship to Creation. The form of the relationship (emotional content) of the experience requires that the learner be able to learn from the teacher that they are valued and have capacity. Knowledge is transferred in the spirit of sharing that takes place in the exchange of knowledge and is the spirit of giving and taking, and the spirit of commitment to the learning process. It is the spirit of the time that is taken to fulfill the learning process. Knowledge is understood to be built through a thoughtful process (capacity to process information for meaning to be reflexive and reflective) that takes place about what is learned. (Mac Saulis)

Individual Racism

Attitudes and actions by individual persons that discriminate and/or oppress others on the basis of their race. It is important to note however that, while an individual can hold racist views and act in a racist manner, these ideas and actions take place in a context that teaches and supports them (not necessarily publicly). (Bill Lee)

Institutional Racism

Refers to discriminatory racial practices built into such prominent structures as political, economic, and educational systems. Institutional racism takes three forms. First, there are instances where practices are based on explicitly racist ideas. For example, Japanese-Canadians were forcibly expelled from British Columbia and had their property confiscated during WWII. Second, there are circumstances where institutional practices arose from, but are no longer sustained by, racist ideas. For example, the migrant-labour policy of admitting black Caribbean workers into Canada during the summer months to work on the farms has its roots in racist thinking – that black workers were racially suited to labour under the hot sun, but not to cold Canadian winters – but, racist ideas are no longer used to justify this migration stream. The third form of institutional racism is commonly referred to as 'systemic discrimination.' For example, the requirement for a certain level of academic performance for admittance to a university overlooks the poorer educational opportunities afforded many aboriginal students. (See Systemic Discrimination) (Brym, 1998: 220)

Interest Group (also known as Pressure Group)

An organization established to influence governmental policy or legislators in a specific area of policy. Examples of special interests might include: a corporation lobbying to win a specific government contract; an entire industry seeking favourable tax policies or government regulations; and groups representing various sectors or interests of society, such as trade unions, senior citizens or persons with disabilities. Special interest groups seek to influence government without becoming part of government. The Right, particularly in North America, has been adept at portraying progressive groups as special interest organizations but as we can see by the array of examples, interest groups are a natural phenomenon in a democratic society. (Bill Lee)

Never doubt that a small group of thoughtful committed individuals can change the world.
Indeed it is the only thing that ever has.
- Margaret Mead

Internal Colonialism

A form of internal oppression, specific to the belief that oneself and one's social group are backward or pathological in key aspects of individual and social life (work ethic or intelligence or ability to govern for example) arising from the imposition of a colonizing society's values and culture. The result is a belief that the oppressed need the governance of the colonizer group. It attributes individual and group problems exclusively to inherent characteristics and discounts the effect of imperial or colonial oppression. In essence it is self blame and says, "If we were better (smarter, more sophisticated, etc.) or more like the dominant group, we would not face the problems we have." It is a form of self-hatred as it alienates (See Alienation) us from the strengths to be found in one's own culture. Aboriginal writers and healers, for example, point to the existence of internal colonialism, resulting from negative media portrayals and the separation of children from their communities as a root cause of many community and individual problems. (Bill Lee)

Internalized Oppression

Refers not only to the belief that one's self and one's social group are inferior, but also encompasses the behaviours that are self-harming and contribute to one's own oppression. These self-destructive behaviours reinforce the dominant group's feelings of superiority, and, in turn, often confirm the oppressed group's feelings of inferiority. Internalized oppression is key to maintaining oppression in that (1) people mistrust themselves and members of their group, which leads to divisiveness; (2) oppressed groups learn to behave without attracting attention or provoking retaliation; and (3) oppressed groups often oppress other oppressed groups to feel superior themselves. Internalized oppression can be reinforced by social workers who focus on personal pathology as the cause of a negative self-image and ignore structural and systemic factors. (Mullaly, 2002: 124)

Internalized Racism

Similar to internalized oppression, internalized racism is the process in which individuals who experience racism adopt the beliefs and attitudes of the dominant group about themselves and about others of their race. (Sheila Sammon)

Intersectionality

The idea of intersectionality suggests that social relations are not only multifaceted and multilayered but also interwoven and mutually constitutive to one another. For instance, poverty is a class phenomenon that is often racialized and gendered. While youth unemployment appears to be a global reality, research shows racialized youth living in working class neighbourhoods are disproportionately disadvantaged in job markets.

Intersectionality is a pivotal conceptual tool to challenge three prevailing problematic notions of difference. First, foundationalism that gives primacy to a particular social relation and dismisses others as secondary or merely manifestation of false consciousness – e.g. orthodox Marxist conception of class or ethnic absolutist understanding of race. Second, relativist parallelism that sees differences only coexisting rather than intertwined. It separates intersecting social struggles from one another. Third, competing marginality focuses on divisive and antagonistic tendencies between different oppositional movements.

In contrast, intersectionality underscores the inseparable interconnectedness between various power relations and social struggles. It points to two strategic foci of anti-oppressive practice: First, locating a common zone of defense – space that connects individuals and communities of various salient issues and concerns. Second, identifying strategic allies and forging short term and long term coalitions for social change. (Rick Sin)

Knowledge

The concept of knowledge is closely related to the notion of truth. Because there may be little agreement about what is true, there is also debate about whether it can be known and become "knowledge." The debate about knowledge not only hinges on whether there are absolute truths that can be known, but on the relationship between truth and power. Is what one regards as truth a reflection of something that is absolute, or a reflection of the power someone has to make us think something is so? Those operating from an anti-oppressive perspective do not necessarily reject all claims that there are absolute truths, yet they will usually subject claims of knowing such truth to critical appraisal. (Gary Dumbrill)

Labour movement

The labour movement is a term used to describe the organization of working people to collectively defend their economic, social and political interests within a class-based society, primarily through legally certified trade unions which bargain collective agreements on behalf of employees in a single or multiple workplace or sector. In Canada, workers have the legal right to join unions and strike when their collective agreement expires. In 2009, approximately 4.6 million Canadian workers belonged to unions in Canada, about 30% of the paid labour force. The influence and interests of the labour movement in Canada extend well beyond narrowly based workplace issues. By engaging in both direct job action and political campaigns, unions remain the most important force for wealth redistribution in capitalist economies. Unions have been instrumental in winning many important forms of social protection for all Canadians, including universal health care, paid holidays, public pensions, unemployment insurance, and health and safety legislation. Despite an on-going assault by neoliberal corporations and policy makers, particularly since the 1970s, union membership today continues to make small gains. During the past several decades, unions across North America have engaged in an important effort to 'renew' their social movement roots by reaching out to under-represented groups such as youth, workers of colour and immigrants, and engaging in community-based coalitions and campaigns. (Janet Dassinger)

Laissez-faire

'Laissez-faire,' from the French, means to leave things alone or not interfere. The notion came to be championed by economists like George Stigler and Milton Friedman and enunciates an economic/political position that holds that human beings are to be understood essentially as economic traders who engage in free, voluntary exchange for mutual benefit and it is best to avoid interfering with this natural system. Thus, government regulation should be limited so that people or organizations can pursue their perceived economic self-interest in whatever way suits them and this will result in the most efficient economic and social systems which will then result in the most benefit to humanity. It is often favoured by right wing ideologues, particularly libertarians (see Libertarianism below). It is critiqued from a range of positions, socialist or spiritual; for example, for a naiveté in ignoring the misery unfettered market approaches have caused (see the industrial revolution and the Great Depression of the 1930s for example). It is also critiqued for the apparent hypocrisy whereby government is encouraged to interfere with social and political activity; for example under the vicious dictator Augusto Pinochet in Argentina. (Bill Lee)

Left Wing

A spatial metaphor derived from seating in the Assembly, a parliamentary body that was part of the government of France during the period of the French Revolution. The further left a person sat, the more she favoured radical measures of redistributing property to poorer people and undoing the power of the monarchy and nobility. Since then, the core of The Left has come to be associated with socialist and communist movements. More generally, it stands for an emphasis on human equality and takes the view that rights to survival and physical well being supersede property rights. The Left-wing is more inclined (than the right) to make systemic changes to strive for economic equality, to push for strengthened state power in the economic sphere, to push to reduce state power in the sphere of personal liberties, to view the world in structural terms and to value collective over individual activity. (See Right- Wing) (Garner, 1991: 20-22; Lee, 2011, Glossary)

LGBTTQI

LGBTTQI is an acronym for the terms Lesbian, Gay, Bisexual, Trans, Two-Spirited, Queer, Intersex. The personal/social identities are presented as a list to acknowledge that the definition of gendered and sexualized identities are social and historical in nature. It is an important acronym in that it acknowledges diversity and counters the tendency to homogenize identity which has been so destructive to queer communities. The list changes according to shared social awareness of identities that have been so repressed that at times they have been rendered invisible. This list is defined by openness and change. It is based on the assumption that the definition of identity is multi-faceted; the possibilities of gender/ sexual social expressions are only as limited as the social imagination. This acronym reminds us that sexualities and genders are multiple and that the binary of male/female or straight/gay is not adequate to understand them. (Ken Moffatt)

Liberalism

Linked to Enlightenment beliefs in the dignity of the individual, freedom of religion, thought and speech and the notion that human beings are progressing through education and technological development. A political/economic doctrine that equates capitalism with freedom and distrusts the power of governments, it stresses liberty as the primary social good, and the defence of rights such as free political institutions, free religious practices, freedom of expression, equal standing before the law and the right to private property. There is a distrust of the state that interferes with such freedoms and with the economy as Liberalism emphasizes freedom of the market, a minimal role for the state, and unrestricted rights for private corporations. Liberalism makes 6 assertions: 1) individual self-interest, when left unchecked, will unconsciously promote the common good; 2) profits are the best incentive for innovation and efficiency, and hence there should be no limit on the accumulation of capital; 3) government power is a threat to freedom in the marketplace, which hinders human freedom; 4) productive firms are best separated from unproductive firms by the dynamics of the free market; 5) nations and independent political communities are barriers to economic progress; and, 6) underdeveloped countries will develop as long as economic factors are allowed to flow freely throughout the world. (Brym, 1998: 253-54; Bullock: 1977: 479)

> *If a free society cannot help the many who are poor, it cannot save the few who are rich.*
> **- J. F. Kennedy (1917-1963)**

Liberation

The freeing of a person or group from restrictive social conventions, an oppressor, or an enemy occupation. An important component of working with an oppressed person or persons is the process of liberation. Although there is no definitive model of liberation, the following attends to the general direction of anti-oppression. First, the oppressed see their oppression in structural terms. Some may respond with anger and demands for change, while others may attempt to pacify and appease the dominant group. Second, they begin to develop a personal sense of identity, pride and self-respect. The final stage occurs when both the dominant and oppressed groups acknowledge that people are taught through socialization to act in oppressive and subordinate ways. This stage will occur only when all groups recognize the interconnectedness of different oppressions and participate in the process of liberation. (Oxford, 1998: 825; Mullaly, 2002: 182-184)

Then surely it is braver, a saner and truer thing, to be a rebel in act and deed against such circumstances as these than tamely to accept it as the natural lot of men.
- Roger Casement, Irish Patriot

Libertarianism

Libertarians argue that people should be free to do whatever they wish as long as it does not interfere with the liberty of others. Libertarians propose a minimal government with little regulation of any kind so that people are "free" to seek their destinies with little inhibition. Libertarianism spans the political spectrum with those on the left opposing people holding private property and other resources because this interferes with the liberty of others, and those on the right arguing that the right to own and control property and resources is a key aspect of liberty. In between these views the libertarian concept is taken up from a number of divergent political and social perspectives. (Gary Dumbrill)

Marginalization

A form of oppression that excludes whole groups of people from useful and meaningful participation in society leading to material deprivation and is a basic feature of injustice and oppression. Though often present, even without material deprivation people may be marginalized, for example, people of colour, old and young people, many single mothers and their children, people with disabilities, unskilled workers and Aboriginal people. These groups constitute a growing underclass permanently confined to the margins of society because the labour market cannot or will not accommodate them. For example, a person with a disability may be marginalized through being treated as unintelligent and unproductive. (Mullaly, 2002: 43-44)

Marxist Social Work

Rooted in an analysis that understands class divisions and exploitation of working people as the centre of alienation and the cause and maintenance of social problems, Marxist social workers attempt to assist people to make the connections between their personal difficulties and this structured inequality. The focus is then on helping people to form groups to examine and take action on their problems and on advocacy (individual and collective) as a primary social work intervention. (Bill Lee)

Marxism

An economic and political philosophy originating in the works of Karl Marx and Friedrich Engels. It characterizes capitalism as inherently exploitive of the mass of the population. In Marxism, society is not built on co-operative relationships, but on inequality and exploitation, and, thus, people cannot reach their full human potential. The economic base of a society is seen as shaping its superstructure – its political, religious, legal and other non-economic institutions. The class with economic power (the bourgeoisie) moulds all social institutions to reinforce its power. Marxism predicts capitalism's inevitable demise because such an exploitative structure is unstable. Marx asserted that eventually the exploited majority (the proletariat) would overthrow their exploiters because capitalism rests on a basic contradiction: production is social – it requires the work of many, while appropriation is private – a small group of people claim the profits. Marx believed that this contradiction would eventually be massive enough to induce a revolution whereby a capitalist society would be replaced by a classless society (first based on socialism and later communism) that shares ownership of the means of production, and exists without a state apparatus. While we may reject the determinism in Marxism it remains a powerful analytical framework for understanding inequality and oppression. (Bullock, 1977: 505; Brym, 1998: 494-496)

Métis

The Métis Nation of Ontario provides the following definition of Métis: The Métis are a distinct Aboriginal people with a unique history, culture, language and territory that includes the waterways of Ontario, surrounds the Great Lakes and spans what was known as the historic Northwest. The Métis Nation is comprised of descendants of people born of relations between Indian women and European men. The initial offspring of these unions were of mixed ancestry. The genesis of a new Aboriginal people called the Métis resulted from the subsequent intermarriage of these mixed ancestry individuals. Distinct Métis settlements emerged as an outgrowth of the fur trade, along freighting waterways and watersheds. In Ontario, these settlements were part of larger regional communities, interconnected by the highly mobile lifestyle of the Métis, the fur trade network, seasonal rounds, extensive kinship connections and a shared collective history and identity. (www.metisnation.org)

The term Métis usually refers to a particular group, primarily the Aboriginal-French descendants of the fur trade era, those who developed their own ethnicity and language in Western Canada. Today the term is used throughout Canada and increasingly in the United States to identify any mixed-Aboriginal/non-Aboriginal person. The use of this term in a generic way is controversial.

Métis, like other Aboriginal peoples are not one homogenous group. Cultural and linguistic differences divide us as surely as geographic distance. The Métis are individuals, groups, and communities indigenous to almost every part of Canada. Most of these peoples have histories and cultures which are often parallel to, but distinct from the development of the Red River Métis communities and those Métis communities so thoroughly documented by past governments in Canada. Métis are not one narrowly bounded, antiquated community which can be easily known, understood, contained and managed. Métis live and coexist within shifting modes and degrees of identity, definition and cultural discovery. More important even than our political and linguistic differences are the things we concern ourselves with as Aboriginal people; such as the turn of the seasons, the telling of how we came to be and what will be our shared fate as living beings on this earth. (Carole Leclair)

Middle-Class

With the development of capitalism, a distinction was drawn between the more powerful and wealthier capitalists (upper class), and smaller capitalists (middle class). The middle class is a group of 'white-collared' salaried workers who are, because of their education and type of work, typically more strongly allied with the elites than with the working class. It is a heterogeneous group, but unity tends to be seen in educational standards, standard of living, ideals of family life and recreational interests. (Fairchild, 1970: 198)

Minority

A group of people, or a member of a group, distinguished by common ties of descent, race, gender, culture and religion. A minority group is (sometimes) smaller than, and less powerful than the controlling group, and is regarded as different from the majority of the population. In modern usage, the term tends to refer to real, threatened, or perceived discrimination against minorities. Some groups can be referred to as *visible minorities*, and they are identified in the

Canada Charter of Rights & Freedoms, for example, as Blacks or South Asians. (Barker, 1987: 99; Bullock, 1977: 533; Wong, 2002: 32)

Misogyny

Misogyny is a term derived from the Greek misogynia, which is a combination of misein- to hate and gyne -woman. It can have various shades of meaning starting with the hatred of women as a group but can also suggest suspicion, dislike or mistrust of women. Its first known use was in the second half of the 17th century. It typically applies to the negative attitude of men toward women, but can also be applied to women who dislike other women in general. Misogyny can be an advantage to men who wish to continue the male domination of power (see Patriarchy). This results in the oppression of women in reducing their access to decision making. Misogyny is found in philosophy, religion, literature and popular culture. One example is found in Greek mythology, the story of Pandora's Box. When Pandora's curiosity gets the best of her, she opens her box and unleashes evil in the form of illness, old age and death into the world. An even more famous example is from the Old Testament where Eve allows the snake to tempt her and then she goes on to tempt the man, Adam. (Cecelia Lee)

Modernism

Refers to a perspective which holds that truth and knowledge exist as objective reality (as do morality and beauty) that can be discovered, examined, understood, and explained through rational and scientific means and then controlled, used and exploited for the betterment of the human condition. Like postmodernism, it is a perspective that attempts to understand the world and our experience of it; but it is a rival perspective to postmodernism. (See Postmodernism) (Mullaly, 2002: 17)

Multiculturalism

Refers to the approach to racial and ethnic diversity that purports to value the differences found among various groups of people. Racism and ethnocentrism are seen as learned attitudes which can be overcome by formal and informal educational interventions. Thus, groups are encouraged to celebrate their particular cultural practices. It has been criticized for ignoring structural barriers that place non mainstream cultures at systematic disadvantage and which require a more fundamental social change than education can afford. (Bill Lee)

Narrative

A story created by a person, family or community where events, interactions and experiences are selectively recalled, arranged and interpreted. The story serves to organize and give meaning to the person, family or community. (Kilpatrick and Holland, 1999: 235)

Narrative Approach/Therapy

A post-modern approach that views problems as stories that people tell themselves. It recognizes that social and political influences and constraints affect people's lives and contribute to or create their problem-saturated stories. Though the amount of direction by the social worker varies, the narrative worker listens to client-generated stories and helps the client to deconstruct and restructure the stories or to explore new possibilities for the stories. Although seen as a practice approach compatible with an anti-oppressive perspective and one that recognizes the social construction of personal problems, its externalizing and questioning techniques can be (mis)used in a manner that ignores the social structures that cause or contribute to personal problems. The narrative approach can be applied to work with individuals, families and communities. It has been used with First Nations communities to honour their histories of resistance and resilience. (see Social Construction) (Franklin & Jordan, 1999: 428. Kilpatrick and Holland, 1999:175) (Sheila Sammon)

Narratives

Stories based on the norms and expectations of larger cultural groups. Narratives are cultural tales that set parameters for what stories are possible. (Biever, Gardner & Bobele, 1999: 153)

We create knowledge so that we can better understand the meaning of our own experience and identity and the complexity of the society in which we live. It is a process of understanding who we are and determining how we want to be. Knowledge should help us to understand our current experience and to develop alternative ways of living that respond to the issues identified.
— **Susan McGrath, Activist and Teacher**

Neo-Colonialism

Broadly, this refers to any and all forms of control of the ex-colonies. In a wider sense the term has come to signify the inability of so-called Third World, or developing or southern economies, to develop an independent economic and political identity under the pressures of globalization. More specifically, it relates to the policy and practice of countries who have achieved technical independence. The ex-colonial powers and the newly emerging superpowers such as the US continue to play a decisive role through international monetary bodies, through the fixing of prices on world markets, multinational corps and cartels and a variety of educational and cultural institutions. Prevalent in discussions of African affairs, and in Latin American and South Asian circles. (Jan Johnstone)

Neo-Conservatism

A movement, and an American term, utilized by individuals of whom many were left-wing radicals who became disillusioned by the Stalinist model of communism or revolted by cultural shifts in America in the 1960s and 1970s. Neo-conservatives believe that concentrating authority within the state is dangerous. They defend capitalism as an imperfect, but manageable system. They value the defense of liberty over the pursuit of equality and tend to distrust the welfare state. They object to government action taken on behalf of minority groups as this is viewed as violating commitments to individualism. They also tend to see the need for a collective national identity that tolerates variety and emphasizes religion and family as sources of social stability. It is an ideology that tries to explain the world in terms of individual desire and initiative, which denies the importance of social relationships and suggests that the world will be best built by individuals pursuing their own interests. (Bullock, 1977: 570; Lee, 2011: Glossary)

Neo-Liberalism

An offshoot of liberal ideology that concentrates on the separation of the government and the economy, its main theme centres around the virtues of laissez-faire capitalism – a capitalist system in which state intervention is minimized. This new focus of liberalism, called neo-liberalism, is predominantly favoured by business people and entrepreneurs who do not want their enterprises regulated. Its guiding image is the free market as the emphasis is on limiting the role of the state in the economy. (See Liberalism, Free Market) (Garner, 1996:136)

A hungry man is not a free man.
— **Adlai Stevenson (1900-1965)**

Neo-Marxism

A term used to refer mainly to post-WWII developments in Marxism. Neo-Marxists are concerned with two key 20th century problems for Marxists: (1) Why was the Soviet Union not a model society? (2) Why has a communist revolution not occurred in advanced capitalist societies as Marx anticipated? With regard to the first question, Neo-Marxists have suggested that the communist party collectively controlled the means of production making them the new dominant class that exploited the rest of society. Communist societies could then be seen as state capitalist societies. The second problem concerning the strength of Capitalism in the west is explained by its imperialism. The West has found new markets and new people to exploit in the Third World. The gains from exploiting those nations enable Western capitalists to buy off their own working-class, while Third World societies are now trapped at the bottom of an international world order. (Brym, 1998: 498) As well, thinkers like Antonio Gramsci (in the 1920s) had pointed to the control that the bourgeois exercised over key institutions like the media, education and military. Thus they formed and managed public discourse that framed understandings of political, social and economic issues and problems such that the masses tended to accept as given the oppressive system in which they lived (See Communism, Marxism, Imperialism). (Bill Lee)

Objectivity/Objectivism

Objectivity explains the relationship between social actors. Objectivity/objectivism assumes an outside social world or reality that exists independent of the actors or subjects. The main epistemological assumption of objectivity is that both social and natural worlds are independent from subjects' interpretations and perceptions. Positivistic sociology, for example, assumes an objectivistic approach to the study of social problems as "things." People and populations are treated as objects that can be studied in a rationalistic, unbiased, value free and impartial way. Disciplines like social work, law, and psychology assume that practitioners are able to practice objectivity. By attempting to keep values outside the interactions between services' users and professionals, workers are, often unwittingly, trying to reduce the human aspect of interaction. There have been many critics of the objective approach in social sciences, particularly feminist, anti-colonialist and poststructuralist philosophers. Authors in these fields have criticized the concept that there is an objective world outside language, institutional interpretations and professional interpretations. They make the point that social locations of subjects (race, gender, sexual orientation, class, disability) as intersecting forces affect the way subjects interact with the social world by constructing, revising, and transgressing it. (Henry Parada)

Ontological

Refers to the branch of philosophy that deals with being. For example, if we talk about something ontologically we are discussing it in terms of what it is in itself. (Laurel Curley)

Oppression

Refers to inhuman and/or degrading treatment of individuals or groups brought about by the dominance of one group over another. It is a process through which individuals or groups unjustly use their power to limit the lives, experiences and opportunities of others with less power. It is a dynamic process that is integrated into a society's institutional order, culture, and the consciousness of its people through socialization by key societal institutions (for example, education and media). Oppression never occurs in isolation; it involves multiple levels that intersect on the basis of age, race, sexual orientation, ability, class and ethnicity. Oppression involves disregarding the rights of an individual or group and is thus a denial of their citizenship. Furthermore, its intensity is not constant; it often changes in response to significant events and social action/movements. Young developed four categories of oppression: exploitation, marginalization, powerlessness and cultural imperialism. (See Discrimination) (Wolfson, 2002: 19; Young, 1990, cited in Wolfson, 2002)

Power in defense of freedom is greater than power on behalf of tyranny and oppression.
– Malcolm X (1925-1965)

Other

Refers to the attempt to form a personal or group identity. We compare ourselves to others and come to understand ourselves as separate and different from others. Although this process of comparison is useful to establishing an identity, it can also create a sense of superiority and an objectification of those who are "different." This is particularly problematic when the "other" is seen or defined as less valuable or when negative characteristics are attributed to the person or group. (Sheila Sammon)

Participative (Participatory) Democracy

Participative Democracy (PD) has emerged as a range of political strategies and practices that seek to involve all members of a population (workers, students, and community members, the so-called 99%) to deliberate, and make decisions that can effectively influence public policy with the ultimate aim of transforming unequal political systems. (Alford & Friedland, 1985, Cohen, J., 2003, Fung & Wright, 2003) PD confronts the concept of mainstream Representative Democracy (RD) that has confined democracy to the vote (Lee, 2011) and bureaucratic administration, integral to liberal capitalist political systems. PD asserts that RD has become extremely weak in advancing democratic ideals of social, political and economical equality. PD proponents draw even mainstream economic thinkers (Stiglitz, 2012) to argue that representative democracy has become a political support of neo-liberal agendas of privatization, deregulation, and reduction of social services and regulatory processes; they note that inequality has become ever deeper and more pervasive (Stiglitz, 2012) and that more and more RD seems to effectively represent only the few wealthier powerful families, and transnational corporations. Thus, PD seeks not only for an authentic and equal political participation for citizens, but also to confront power relations and subordination.

Examples of PD include the Occupy movement, Homeless Movement in Brazil, Iceland revolution against the financial crisis, Real Democracy Now (Democracia real Ya) in Spain, participatory city budgeting process in Porto Alegre, Brazil and the Neighborhood councils for education in Chicago, USA. (Martha Lara)

Government should be defined as a group of men who are put in place by financiers and
industrialists to take the blame when the financiers and industrialists ruin the economy.
– (Rev.) Edward Lee CSB

Paternalism

Protection and control, like that of a minor child by a parent, exercised by the government over the governed, employer over employee, or in similar relationships. It is a principle of authority in which one person or institution manages the affairs of another. The term is often used disparagingly against social workers and social welfare organizations that try to help people solve their problems without the direct involvement of those being 'helped,' hence, Alinsky's famous definition of social worker: a person who helps people live in hell and like it. (Fairchild, 1970: 214; Barker, 1987: 117)

Patriarchy

Derived from the Greek 'rule of the father,' it describes authority and control exercised by men over women. Patriarchy may refer to both a state of affairs, control in institutions, and an ideology (embedded in a culture's language). (Bullock, 1977: 632)

I'll be a post feminist in the post patriarchy
– bumper sticker

Pedagogy

At its most simple level this term refers to the teaching or study of teaching or education. In more critical frame however it refers to the existence of oppressive and hierarchical relations and narratives embedded within and reproduced by formal educational processes and institutions (media, education and church for example). The process of "teaching" may be subtle or overt but in whatever form these institutions serve to maintain the status quo of the social and economic hierarchy. On the other hand Freire (2000) asserts that it is possible and imperative to develop a counter pedagogy, one that will both expose the oppressive nature of the institutional pedagogy and assist the oppressed to interrogate their own situation and that of the wider social, political and economic contexts and in this way discover, analyze and act to change the world. (Bill Lee)

Pluralism

In general, this is a position that affirms and accepts diversity, founded on qualities of mutual respect and tolerance. Theorists like Isaiah Berlin suggest that in politics, the affirmation of diversity in the interests and beliefs of the citizenry is one of the most important features of modern democracy. The term is also used, in several different senses, in the context of religion and philosophy. It is an approach that allows for individuals to choose their own sets of beliefs and values, and suggests the notion of dialogue and serious thought in seeking the common good. Critics contend that a naive acceptance of the notion of pluralism within a globalizing world ignores very real culture and class divides which interfere with mutual respect and tolerance. Others such as Wendy Brown argue that an uncritical acceptance of notions such as pluralism allow for the unfettered reproduction or maintenance of dominant discourse and social power relations. (Bill Lee)

Political

Refers primarily to the social discourse focused on the formal laws and regulations by which a society governs itself in issues relating to the public sphere of life. Thus, legislatures make laws on and regulate various aspects of life like taxes, road safety, etc. Also, it refers to issues concerning the manner in which power and resources are distributed or managed in a state, community or organization. For example, when individuals act in such a manner that their opportunities for promotion in an organization or influence in a community are enhanced, they are said to be acting in a political manner. (Bill Lee)

Political Correctness

Careful and sensitive use of language to avoid using terms that might hurt, marginalize or exclude people who are not of a dominant social group. An example might be when we use a term like "people with disabilities" as opposed to "disabled people." The term is often used negatively by those who wish to criticize or dismiss comments by people who are attempting to challenge social norms, language and actions that perpetuate stereotypes and contribute to oppression. An example here might be when one is "charged" with being politically correct for challenging someone who is making a racist comment or telling a joke that is sexist. (Sheila Sammon)

Popular Education

Suggests that people are at the center of the creation of their own education. Education is seen as a critical instrument or process that can be used for either subjugation or liberation. This, for example, is why government and churches deprived Native communities of their education function for so long. Popular education depends on dialogue, and rejecting the assumption that people are empty vessels into which knowledge is poured. Oppressed people have been taught to devalue their own experience and knowledge, and not to see the processes that have made them the objects of oppressive systems. People have old and new experiences that can be used to identify the roots of problems, information they already know, and what they need to learn to organize and confront oppressive systems. (See Dialogue) (New Internationalist, 2002: 19; Freire, 2000; Lee, 2011: 58)

Populism

An ideology and a type of mobilization. It is sometimes associated with left-wing movements, but is an ambiguous activism and there is considerable disagreement about its place in the spectrum of movements. Populism means an ideology of, or for, the people. It is a view and a movement that calls for mobilization against the rich and powerful in the name of the people. Populist discourse is strongly 'anti-elitist.' Populism is not currently a movement with a coherent ideology like the varieties of liberalism or socialism; it is an element within movement ideologies, or a mode of operating, rather than a definable movement. It promises a better life, less economic inequality and more political involvement for the people. The ambiguity of the term 'the people' has allowed populist movements to take on many forms and goals. For example, fascist and Nazi movements may use elements of populist thought. (See Elite, Ideology and Fascism) (Garner, 1991:185)

Positivism

Positivism is the approach to science (to generating knowledge) of the natural sciences. It is based on a theory of reality that holds that facts exist 'out there,' separate from our ideas or perceptions. Laws of human behaviour and human relations are there to be discovered (mostly by observation and experimentation). Positivism also claims that researchers can and should be objective: they can and should conduct studies that are uninfluenced by the researcher's values or circumstances, culture, historical time, or social location. Post-positivists also believe that there is a reality independent of human perception, but differ from positivists in asserting that our knowledge of this reality is affected by our social location and experience. They draw on many different sources of knowledge, towards an always-imperfect description of reality. (Christina Sinding)

Post-Modernism

Proposes that truth, beauty, morality, and social life have no objective reality beyond how we think, talk, and write about them. Like modernism, it is a perspective that attempts to understand the world and our experience of it; however, it is a rival perspective to modernist thought. Post-modernism has been especially important in acknowledging the multiple forms of 'otherness' as they emerge from differences in subjectivity, gender, class and race. It helps the anti-oppressive worker develop a new politics of solidarity – one that always gives attention to the differences within particular oppressed groups. (See Modernism) (Mullaly, 2002: 17 & 25)

> *Objectivity is defined as a distanced external view "uncoloured by feelings or opinions." Taken to its logical conclusions, it is the absence of a point of view. But everyone ... has a point of view and feelings or opinion that are impossible to set aside completely.*
> **– Jan Barnsley and Diana Ellis, Feminist Researchers**

Post-Structuralism

This is a post-modern social theory originating in France in part as a response to structuralism. Post-structuralists – for example Michel Foucault and Jacques Derrida – are engaged by Sassure's argument that language gains meaning through a relationship to other words rather than as a transparent reflection of the concrete world (see Structuralism). However, post-structuralists such as Derrida challenge structuralism by arguing that the notion of structures relies on a belief that there is a "stable centre" – that is, a way of seeing the world that is normal and universally agreed upon, from which everything else deviates. Post-structuralists argue that the centre usually reflects the values and interests of powerful groups in society. For example, they see the meaning of masculinity as being secured through competing discourses which are not all equal; some are dominant while others are marginalized. The accepted or dominant definition of masculinity is understood as one that protects the interests of the most powerful groups in society. So, Post-structuralists argue that there are no universal rules of masculinity. What is acceptable or normal is always determined by the dominant discourses within a community or society. Post-structuralism is a critique of the ways in which these types of signs and discourses are chosen, so that certain relations of inequality are maintained. (Sarah Todd)

Poverty

In narrow terms, poverty is generally understood to refer to revenue poverty, that is, a level of household income which falls below some measure of a basic minimum income. Income poverty lines range from an absolute measure of poverty (the cost of basic necessities such as food, shelter and clothing) to relative measures (some percentage of the median income in society), depending on whether the goal is to have access to basic life necessities or to have access to a standard of living that has some relation to the average standard of living in that society. A relative measure of poverty indicates a concern beyond subsistence to equality; and the prevention of growing inequality in the distribution of societal resources.

In broader terms, poverty has important dimensions in addition to income. It can include lack of access to assets and land, social isolation, powerlessness, loss of group and self-esteem, ill health, substandard housing, absence of work or a fair return on one's labour.

Analysis of the causes of poverty ranges from a diagnosis of individual deficiencies on the part of poor persons to an analysis of structural causes found in macro economic policies and the oppressions of race, class, gender, ability, etc. (Stephanie Baker Collins)

Power

Power is understood as the degree to which we are able to influence our environments – to get things done, make things happen (or not happen). It includes access to resources, free choice and opportunity. Without power, individuals cannot participate as citizens and thus become alienated. They are prevented from exercising the appropriate responsibilities and rights in shaping their lives. There are 5 elements of power: 1) money; 2) information (technical, academic, and privileged information occupies a central influencing place in the public's attention, and is mainly controlled by dominant forces such as big business and professionals); 3) numbers (there is extraordinary power in large numbers of people that are organized to make demands); 4) status (which comes from the formal or informal right to act in particular areas or on particular issues, and thus to control the course of particular issues in society); and 5) belief or conviction (referring to a spiritual aspect of life – a sense of purpose higher than simply accepting the circumstances of our lives). (Lee, 2011: 23-27; Wolfson, 2002: 21)

The exercise of power is never neutral.
– Jeremy Rifkin

Praxis

Refers to the unity of theory and practice. Marx claimed that thought or theory cannot be seen as separate from practice, as some abstract standard or contemplative ideal. Rather, it arises out of practice and is developed and modified by it. Marx considered that the split between 'ideal' and 'reality' could only be overcome by the development of a theoretical consciousness among those engaged in the practice of changing the 'real' world. The praxis of the masses would, therefore, consist in the growth of a socialist consciousness arising out of the conditions of their lives and their attempts to transform them. Paulo Freire asserts that no reality transforms itself; therefore, the people must be engaged in the fight for their own liberation through praxis. (Bullock, 1977: 680; Freire, 2000: 53)

Prejudice

Refers to a set of biased and generalized beliefs (stereotypes) about people, derived largely from inaccurate and incomplete information. Although prejudice can be seen as part of an individual's belief system, it is also a social phenomenon that originates when the dominant groups attempt to ideologically justify and entrench their power and privilege over others. (Elliott & Fleras, 1992: 334)

Pressure Group (See Interest Group)

Privilege

Refers to advantage not available to others on equal terms. It may entail unfair advantage sanctioned by law or based upon power and exploitation. Usually, it is used as an adverse term, applied when privileges are used as a means of further exploitation, or to grasp more power and privilege. Privilege also refers to having control of a society's surplus resources. Bases of privilege include sex, race, age, ability and other dimensions of oppression. (Fairchild, 1970: 234; Brym, 1998: 184)

Queer Theory

Queer theory is a philosophical and theoretical position that has renewed understanding of identity and politics for people who have been marginalized due to their sexuality. Queer theorists reject dichotomous structures for understanding sexuality such as gay versus straight. In addition queer theorists reject a simple oppositional structure to politics of sexuality that assumes a minority group fights against a heterosexual norm. Rather queer theorists are interested in a multiplicity of sexualities and genders and are interested in celebrating how this diversity of sexualities exists without the permission of a dominant class of persons. Building on the historical work of gay liberation and feminist theorists, queer theorists have revitalized the politics of sexuality. They assume that there is no essential nature to being a man or woman; but rather, gender and sexuality, like other identities are constructed through social relations and discourses. Queer theorists argue that the politics of gender and sexuality exist in our daily practices since our identities are constructed through language and practices. The use of the term queer in queer theory is an example of how derogatory prejudicial language can be reconstructed. Queer persons have taken the word and reclaimed it as their own so that what was once hurtful language is a mark of pride. Queer theory challenges our basic assumptions of categories of gender, sexuality and the power relations between men and women. Through this challenge we are open to construct new identities and reconstruct troubling gender, and sexual social relations. (Ken Moffatt)

Race

Most commonly used to divide individuals into categories based on physical differences, such as skin colour, shape of facial features, and texture of hair. It was widely believed that races were real and objective subdivisions of humans until the 1950s when scientific consensus was that racial classifications are arbitrary, and socially constructed typologies. Although race is a hollow biological concept, many people organize their relationships, behaviour and attitudes as though it were not. The concept becomes important when physical differences are attributed to nonphysical features such as abilities, aptitudes, and emotions. Hence, the effect of the concept is very real and important in modern society. (Brym, 1998: 218)

Racialized Groups

Groups who have been assigned a 'race' category – e.g., black, Latino, Native American – through the use of racist discourses. Racialization processes in North America and Europe have used discourses of whiteness as standards of measure to assess or classify other groups. White standards and judgements create a hierarchy of those who are accepted or included and those who are excluded from power as well as to what degree. That is, they are arbitrarily assigned various personal and social traits and at the same time – sometimes subtly, sometimes clearly – restricted in terms of life opportunities by the dominant population. Because of this they tend to lack social capital and the power to significantly influence social institutions. (Henry Parada)

Racism

The belief that human qualities and abilities are determined by race and that one race is inherently superior to all others, giving it the right to dominate other races. Underpinning racism is the belief that race is based on biological evidence. For example, a particular skin colour is inherently associated with intelligence. Such racial classifications are social constructs that carry out certain ideological and political functions for the racially privileged group (white). Essentialism is also a part of racism in that there is a belief that everybody classified under a particular race possesses the same characteristics. For example, that all black people are superior at sports and athletics. Although race is a hollow biological concept, racism is not. Through the assumption of racial superiority, racism has had profound negative effects on people of colour within most Eurocentric societies and the countries they have colonized. People of colour are stereotyped, oppressed and discriminated against at the personal, cultural, and structural levels of society. (Mullaly, 2002:162)

God wills us free, man wills us slaves, I will as God wills, God's will be done
– Daniel Bliss (Epitaph on the Gravestone of John Jack, 1773)

Radical

A person or process that aims at understanding and acting on the roots of problems; the process of looking past symptoms by analyzing them. (Lee, 2011, Glossary)

Radical Social Work

Refers to the ideology among some social workers that the most effective way to achieve goals of equality and solutions to social problems is to eliminate or make major changes in existing institutions. Radical social work includes strategies for peaceably bringing about these changes, including nonviolent resistance, demonstrations, strikes, and other political and social activism. (Barker, 1987: 135)

Reclaim / Re-appropriate

Both terms refer to a process where a word or term that has been used as a pejorative against a population has been brought back into acceptable usage by that population as an act of collective resistance and self-empowerment. It is a process that is typically used within communities that have experienced the effect of stereotyping or otherwise negative language as part of the process of oppression and marginalization. Two notable examples: the term Queer has been reclaimed by members of the Lesbian/Gay/Transsexual/Transgendered/Bisexual/Queer groups to identify themselves as a specific collective and culture, while the term Black has been similarly re-appropriated as a positive signifier by Afro-North American groups. (Bill Lee)

Reflexivity

Refers to the phenomenon of self-reference. Reflexivity has raised problems for the status of the social sciences – especially psychology and sociology. These are essentially reflexive because they are generated by and involved in creating their own knowledge. For example, sociology is itself a social institution and its theories provide many of the terms for which social phenomena are understood and acted upon. One lesson learned from reflexivity is that sociologists and psychologists are not external 'objective' observers of the social world, but are active and creative participants in it. (Bullock, 1977: 738-39)

Reform

Reform refers to the improvement in a particular social pattern with special emphasis upon function rather than upon structure. Reform movements aim to alleviate distress and to correct maladjustments without attempting to alter society itself. (Fairchild, 1970: 252-253)

Relativism

Relativism assumes that there are no universal, objective and fundamental truths that can be applied to all realities and circumstances. It assumes that realities are constructed and are determined by social relations within a particular social context. Language plays an important role; not as a medium to understand the world but as a means to construct the world through the attempt to explain it. Although reality may be socially constructed through the use of language, relativism acknowledges the presence of social, economic and other forms of social relations that affect how people experience reality. An extreme form of relativism is Nihilism, a point of view that sees every form of reality construction as acceptable. (Henry Parada)

Representative Democracy

Refers to a political, social and economic system. The size of nations has meant that democracy has been exercised indirectly through the free election of representatives – representative democracy. The criteria of such democracy are that: (1) such elections are free – held frequently, citizens are able to vote, candidates are able to campaign, and voting secrecy is protected; (2) effective choices are provided at elections – more than one party is represented; (3) elected representatives have the right of legislation, the right to control the budget (through majority vote), and the right to publicly oppose, question, and discuss government measures without threats, interference or arrest. These same principles of representative democracy can be applied to other organizations besides the state, such as factories and universities. (Bullock, 1977: 208-209)

Resistance

Refers to a refusal to comply. Foucault argued that power is always faced with resistance, that every exercise of power is contested, and that resistance itself is an act of countervailing power. This idea has enormous potential for anti-oppressive practice. It challenges the view that individuals or subordinate groups are helpless to do anything about the dominant discursive practices that oppress them. Such dominance can be challenged through acts of resistance to undermine oppressive ideas, assumptions and discourses. (Oxford, 1998:127; Mullaly, 2002: 21-22)

Reverse Racism

This expression is used when people from the dominant cultural group feel discriminated against by policies, practices or measures taken to favour non-dominant and minority groups. For example, they argue that racism is occurring in reverse, that is, towards those who are from the dominant cultural group because employers are told to have employment equity policies in their job ads. Consequently, employment equity policies are viewed as discrimination towards those who are from the dominant cultural group since they are not encouraged to apply in the same way as those who come from a minority group. Such claims of 'reverse racism' rest on: a) the premise that equity policies cause the prospects of those from the dominant group to suffer in relation to minority groups; b) a tendency to deny how inequities exist in our systems and institutions; c) a belief that a dominant cultural group does not exist in society and, subsequently, any recognition of inequality should be viewed with suspicion; and (6) a belief that we live in a fundamentally equal society. (June Ying Yee)

Revolution

A sweeping, sudden change in the societal structure, or in some important feature of it – a form of social change distinguished by its scope and speed. When the partisans of change have become more powerful than the established authorities, they assume those positions of authority and substantially alter the social, economic, and political organization of society in their favour. The essence of revolution is the sudden change, not violent upheaval, which frequently accompanies it. Violence that occurs is rather the overt evidence that the change has occurred. (Fairchild, 1970: 259; Brym, 1998: 466)

Rights

Refers to anything that an individual or group is entitled to expect from its social/political environment according to the norms of that society. All rights are socially granted and guaranteed, and they have no existence beyond the extent to which they are socially supported. (Fairchild, 1970: 260)

We have no special right because we belong to one race or another:
the word (human) defines all rights.
- Jose Marti (1815-1895)

Right Wing

A spatial metaphor derived from seating in the Assembly, a parliamentary body that was part of the government of France during the period of the French Revolution. Those sitting on the right favoured protecting existing property rights and undertaking only limited changes in the political system. Since then, the core of the Right-wing has come to be associated with being conservative, less inclined to challenge existing institutions, more convinced that hierarchy and continuity of traditions, rather than equality, are essential in human society, and more sympathetic toward property rights. The Right is generally opposed to having the state do things like regulate business or redistribute tax revenues to equalize economic standing; but some parts of the Right are not opposed to having the state regulate personal behaviour, so it cannot really be said that all of the Right is consistently for less government. For example, restricting access to abortions tends to be a Right-wing policy – this is an area where The Right would like greater state intervention. (See Left Wing) (Garner, 1996: 20-22)

Self

An understanding of and relationship to one's complex identity. According to Foucault, the self is an outcome of historical developments. It is not an essence. Self does not exist outside established forms of knowledge and institutionalized practices. (Chambone, Irving, & Epstein, 1999: 278)

Self-Reflexivity

The act of making oneself an object of one's own observation. In social work, this would include thinking about our past life experiences and our social location and analyzing how these affect our attitudes and the way we act. (Lax, 1992: 75)

Service Users' Knowledge/Theory

Service users' knowledge emerges from the lived experience of those receiving social work interventions. Service users' theory is the ways such service users understand and make sense of their experience. Unlike knowledge and theory developed by social workers, from the delivery end of intervention, the knowledge and theory of service users is developed at the receiving end of intervention. Such theory includes, but is not limited to service users' understanding of their own needs, the reasons they have these needs, the types of service that best meet these needs, and the outcomes and consequences of existing intervention practices. Service users' theory has tended to be ignored by social workers. Traditionally it has been the theories that social workers develop about what service users need which predominate. Recently, however, particularly in Britain, the legitimacy and need to have service users' theory shape intervention has become increasingly recognized. (Gary C. Dumbrill)

Sexism

Refers to a set of social, economic, political, and cultural beliefs, attitudes, and practices that oppress women. Sexism is similar to racism in that each is based on notions of biological determinism and essentialism: the biological differences being, for example, passivity, emotionality, nurturing, irrationality, and weakness; and the essentialist beliefs being that all women possess these characteristics. These characteristics are then used to rationalize the subordination of women. Women are not a homogenous group. Although each woman is oppressed by patriarchy, not every woman is oppressed to the same degree or in the same way: each woman's oppression is mediated by her class, race, and other social characteristics. (Mullaly, 2002: 163-165)

Sexualities

The plural term sexualities is meant to more realistically reflect the nature of sexuality. By being plural the term acknowledges that there are a wide variety of sexualities Sexuality is nuanced and varied according to each person. In fact, a person can have more than one sexuality. The term sexualities removes the restrictive binary of straight/gay and heterosexual/homosexual. Sexualities become possible and are constructed through social relations as much as they are based in individual desire. The term connotes that the idea of two sexes and two sexualities is neither inevitable nor desirable. (Ken Moffatt)

Sexual Orientation(s)

Sexual orientation is becoming an increasingly dated term. However the term has some usefulness, the strength of the term is that it avoids pathologizing a person's sexual desire. The orientation of a person is the focus or direction of one's desire. That is, sexual orientation can be directed to the same sex, opposite sex, or both sexes. Sexual orientation suggests that a person's sexual attraction can change over time since it is an orientation rather than a given entity. Another strength of the term is that it acknowledges that everyone has a sexual orientation and does not problematize one sexual orientation over another. (Ken Moffatt)

Sexual Preferences

Sexual preference suggests that a person can be attracted to more than one gender or sexuality. The person can have a preference rather than a single sexual object of desire. (Ken Moffatt)

Social Citizenship

An understanding of citizenship in which three areas of rights of the modern citizen have been identified: civil, political and social. Civil rights concern individual freedom, including freedom of speech, thought and faith, the right to own property and the right to justice. The political element includes the right to participate in the exercise of political power. The issue of social rights suggest a range of rights, from the franchise to a reasonable level of economic welfare and security to the right to share to the full in the social heritage and to live the life of a civilized being according to the existing standards of society. The measure of social citizenship, then, can be seen as the extent to which an individual as citizen is guaranteed access to the things seen as essential to basic dignity and participation in the society in which she or he lives. (Marshall, 1950:10-11; Morrison, 1997: 69)

Taxes are the price we pay for a civilized society.
– Oliver Wendell Holmes Jr. (1841-1935)

Social Class

Social class refers to people grouped by a social characteristic. Classes are usually conceptualized hierarchically, with powerful elite groups at the top dominating less powerful subordinate groups at the bottom. Classes are often defined along economic lines. Karl Marx, for instance, categorized class based on one's relationship to the means of production, with the two predominant groups being the bourgeoisie who owned the means of production and the proletariat who did not and had to sell labour power to the bourgeoisie to survive. Many other conceptualizations of class based on economics exist, but there are also classifications based on heritage or the ways one acts in society. In ancient Rome, for instance, several classes existed with the patricians occupying the upper position and claiming lineage back to ancient Troy, and the plebeians who could not. This classification was not based on wealth but family history, yet given that the patricians tended to hold power and wealth it was largely synonymous with an economic classification. (Gary Dumbrill)

Social Construction

Refers to the process of defining what is real, and that these judgments are made through interactions among people. Sociologists are interested in which particular groups, such as scientists, doctors and officials in bureaucracies, are able to define the things we believe to be true. (Brym, 1998: 59)

Social Exclusion

Social exclusion is both a process and an outcome that occurs and is experienced both at personal or subjective and macro-societal levels. It is political in nature with oppressions created mainly by inequitable and unjust economically-based forces. As a process, particular groups are marginalized, alienated, ostracized, stigmatized, and disempowered from participating in community and societal processes in full and meaningful ways. Unjust structural, institutional and/or systemic obstacles/barriers are often the mechanisms by which social exclusion is propagated and perpetuated. Subsequently, social exclusion reinforces cleavages and divisions across diversity and heterogeneous interests in a manner that is detrimental to sustainable human development but often conducive to short-term capitalistic objectives. As an outcome, a socially exclusive condition is one in which marginalization, alienation, stigmatization, and disempowerment exist from individual to community to societal levels. Thus, social exclusion underpins many broader negative social phenomena such as poor population health outcomes, various forms of violence and poverty for example. It is self perpetuating in that by its nature it raises barriers to members of society wishing to escape oppression. (Anthony Hutchinson)

Social Inclusion

Social inclusion (like social exclusion) is both a process and an outcome that occurs and is experienced both at personal or subjective and macro-societal levels. As a process, human beings are encouraged, enabled, and empowered to participate in community and societal processes in a full and meaningful way unhindered by structural, institutional and/or systemic obstacles/barriers regardless of political persuasion. Subsequently, social inclusion incorporates pluralism, diversity and heterogeneous interests to the maximum extent in addressing all socially-based realities. In its fullest sense social inclusion is not merely a remedy to address social and/or economic disparities. Nor is it simply about "bringing in" human beings from the margins of society. Rather, it is about the elimination of all barriers and obstacles (economic, political and social) that impede full and meaningful human participation across all societal spheres. Individual agency becomes the sole limitation to such participatory activities at the subjective level based on uncompromised individual choice. In the event where exclusion is deemed appropriate (the criminal justice system or in issues of national security) the justification of such obstacles must be made wholly transparent. As an outcome, the actualization of a socially inclusive community or society is not one of ultimate cohesion or assimilation. Rather, it is one that is governed and represented by processes of respect, reciprocity, sensitivity and anti-oppression. (Anthony Hutchinson)

Socialism

Refers to a social system based on the common ownership of the means of production and distribution (vs. a minority group having ownership). It is an ideology that challenges the basic premises of liberalism. For socialists, inequality in the economic domain inevitably permeates every sphere of society. Unlike liberalism, socialists believe that the private and unequal structure of the economy creates a general situation of inequality that blocks the attainment of individuals' real potential, freedom, and political participation. Socialist ideas were given expression during working class movements that demanded democracy, equality and collectivism. Historically, it has pressed for the extension of universal suffrage (the right to vote), social reforms, improved working conditions, and greater state control over the market and the economy. It is sometimes referred to as the transitional stage between a working class revolution and communism. (See Liberalism, Communism) (Bullock, 1977: 807; Garner, 1996:156)

Socialization

Refers to the learning of knowledge, skills, motivations and identities as our genetic potential interacts with our social environment. This process takes place throughout our lives. Sometimes our self-concept undergoes abrupt change as we quickly learn new roles and a new self-image – this is referred to as *resocialization*, and is most evident in jails and mental health hospitals. (Brym, 1998: 30)

Social Justice

This concept is central to anti-oppressive practice. It is rooted in the understanding of human beings as primarily social in nature and thus that social well-being must be a central concern of society. It is focused on the notion that all persons have a range of fundamental rights that must be respected as part of the public good of society. The word social clearly distinguishes it from the concept of justice as applied in the law. It holds some or all of the following principles: first, historical inequities insofar as they affect current injustices – for example, class, race, gender, sexual orientation, physical/mental ability and culture/national origin – should be corrected until the actual inequities no longer exist or have been perceptively "negated"; second and following on the first, it is crucial that groups have authentic opportunity to voice concerns and perspectives on issues of the public good; third, the redistribution of wealth, power and status for the individual, community and societal good; fourth, it is the responsibility of government (or those who hold significant power) to ensure a basic quality of life for all citizens. (Bill Lee)

Social Location

Refers to the social position (class, race, sexual orientation, ability etc.) one occupies and thus the level of privilege to which we have access. (See Privilege) (Swan, 2003: 39)

Solution Focused Therapy

Solution Focused Therapy would ordinarily not be in an AOP Glossary of Terms other than it is often mistaken as a form of anti-oppressive practice. The approach is compatible with AOP because the worker or therapist takes a "one down position" and recognizes service users as experts of their own lives. The model is also potentially empowering by focusing on solutions and client strengths rather than problems and client pathology. These characteristics are compatible with anti-oppression, but the model tends to assume that clients have the resources to achieve their objectives, and from an anti-oppressive perspective this is clearly not so because a lack of resources caused by social equity is a "problem" many service users face and needs to be addressed by workers. The model can be expanded, however, to recognize social inequalities and to seek solutions to such forms of oppression. (Gary Dumbrill)

Specious

Refers to something deceptive. This is usually an argument or line of reasoning, that appears to be fair, attractive or true but which is actually not so. A position may look good when we first see or hear it but when we look deeper we find that it has serious flaws. For example, trickle down economics was originally accepted on its face value, if the rich are given tax breaks they will spend the money or invest it and everyone will benefit. It is now clear that the rich will often have bought all the consumer goods they desire and that their investments may go into stocks or enterprises which will benefit no one but themselves and their class. (Laurel Curley)

Standpoint Theory

Standpoint theories have their roots in Marxism and socialist feminism. Standpoint theories assume that what we (can) know about the world is deeply connected to 'where we stand' in the world – to our social locations (and in some versions of standpoint theory, especially to the sorts of work we do). Standpoint theories draw attention to how the knowledge that dominant groups have of the world tends to be taken as 'the truth' – even though it is often flawed. Standpoint theories give rise to the idea of epistemic privilege (see epistemic privilege). (Christina Sinding)

State, The

A system of institutions that has the power to govern through the use of laws and regulations, groups of people within particular geographic boundaries. It is the one entity to which people (citizens) cede the right to the use of force in regulating their behaviour. Some would argue that the state is able to articulate the common values and interests of its population. Others would counter that the state expresses only those interests and values that reinforce in the interests of the governing and economic elites. (Bill Lee)

State-Capitalism

A political-economic system whereby the means of production is collectivized and decisions centralized in the state which is governed in the interests of a ruling elite (who reap the profits) rather than the whole body of citizens. For example, what was referred to as communism in the old Soviet Union and other eastern European countries was in reality state capitalism. (Bill Lee)

Status-Quo

The existing situation. In the context of AOP it usually refers to the existing relations and conditions that reflect and perpetuate unequal power relationships. (Bill Lee)

Stereotypes

Refers to a shared consensus regarding the generalized attributes of others with respect to perceived physical, social, emotional or cultural characteristics. Stereotypes involve generalizations extended to all members of the group. Although they may be positive, neutral or negative, they can be harmful when they deny the genuine uniqueness of a person and the diversity that exists within a group. In this case, they can be the foundation upon which racism, discrimination and oppression occurs. (Elliott & Fleras, 1992, Eagleton, 2007)

Structural Analysis

The examination of the fundamental social, economic and political structures which initiate and maintain, over the long term, the concrete conditions under which people, particularly the marginalized, live their lives and the attitudes and values which frame their understandings. For example, we may wish to examine how the media, owned by a narrow band of elites, present the issue of globalization as a natural and normal evolutionary development. The question arises, whose interests are served and whose are ignored by the presentation of such an interpretation? Structural analysis does not aim at development of a specific strategy. Rather, it provides the crucial context in which an immediate strategic or conjunctural analysis can be undertaken. (Naming the Moment Project; Whitmore and Wilson, 1997: 59)

Structuralism

This concept emphasizes the role that societal structures have in shaping human action and identity. It has shaped the fields of anthropology, sociology and linguistics. It is a tradition out of which structural approaches to social work have evolved. These approaches to social work focus on the ways in which social relations of power shape people's personal lives. The most influential work of structuralists has focused on the construction of language and how it determines our subjectivity, or the meaning we give ourselves. Ferdinand de Sassure argued that in any language the relationship between the signifier (the word) and the signified (the object) is arbitrary. For example, there is nothing "doggy" about the word "dog." Signifiers gain their meaning through their relationship to, or difference from, other signifiers within the language system. Structuralists are particularly interested in the signifying relationships that rely on binary oppositions (white/black, man/woman). The arbitrariness and dichotomous nature of language systems are linguistic rules that constrain how we can make sense of ourselves and others. For example, we understand something as feminine if it is not masculine. It becomes difficult not to imagine masculinity and femininity as absolute opposites. Structuralists then, believe that our subjectivity is only possible through language and, as a result, there are limits to the possibilities we have to create ourselves as subjects. So, we have to construct our gender identity in terms of opposition to another gender identity. We are not essentially masculine or feminine, but constitute ourselves as such through language and practice. (Sarah Todd)

Structural Social Work

A model of practice that assumes inadequate social arrangements are primarily responsible for personal problems, and aims to help persons modify the social situation that limits their functioning. For example, rather than solely connecting an unemployed person with a disability to needed resources, a structural social worker would encourage the individual to challenge and change institutions that support and perpetuate their exclusion. (Barker, 1987:159)

Sub-Culture

Distinctive discourses about specialized interests and experiences shared by a network of individuals whose way of life is different from that of the majority of people in their society. Although individuals in a sub-culture may be part of the dominant culture, they hold distinctive values, norms and beliefs. (Brym, 1998: 72)

Symbolic Power and Symbolic Struggle

Symbolic power is the capacity to make a particular way of seeing and understanding the world to become taken-for-granted norms. Symbolic struggle is the process of competing for the imposition of such understanding of the world. Both terms, symbolic struggle and symbolic power, are to be understood in Bourdieu's view of social existence. He sees that social life is a competition for both material and symbolic benefits, but the ultimate competition is for symbolic power, that is the capacity to define reality, because it has a bearing on the accumulation of wealth and material benefits. (Winnie Lo)

Symbolic Violence (from Bourdieu's theory)

Symbolic violence is a concept that unveils the potency of the symbolic dimension of power. Symbolic violence refers to a process in which power is transmitted in such misrecognized forms so that it escapes the awareness of both those who transmit it and those who are impacted by it. Power is misrecognized because it is mediated symbolically so that it masks the inequalities from which it derives its power. Violence alludes to a domination that is based on an arbitrary assignment of distinction to certain qualities and values. Symbolic violence, thus, is the wielding of symbolic power which masks its face of inequalities and arbitrariness. One important implication of the concept is that people participate in their own domination without knowing it. (Winnie Lo)

Systemic Discrimination

Refers to the restriction of life chances of certain groups through a variety of seemingly neutral rules, regulations and procedures. For example, word-of-mouth hiring practices are a form of systemic discrimination in that they deliberately or unintentionally put minority groups at a disadvantage. Companies with poor access for those who use wheel chairs discriminate in systemic terms by limiting their ability to access services or employment. Systemic discrimination can encompass a wide variety of groups: women, gays/lesbians/transgendered/transsexuals, Aboriginal people, people with disabilities, or people of colour, for example. (Brym, 1998: 220)

Systemic Racism

A powerful force that discriminates against minorities at institutional levels. This type of racism is impersonal, unconscious, unintentional, and covert. With systemic racism, it is the consequence (not the intent) of seemingly neutral rules, policies, or procedures that establish its distinctive character. (Elliott & Fleras, 1992: 336)

Tolerance

This is an essentially political term used within debates in areas of social, cultural and religious context. It is proposed as the opposite to discrimination. The term is often used in reference to "foreign" or "other" cultural beliefs and practices, as well as to more particular categories, such as discrimination against unusual sexual and social orientation. It is perhaps exemplified best by former Prime Minister Trudeau's comment, *"There's no place for the state in the bedrooms of the nation."* This implies that society must "tolerate" private action that has no effect on the public sphere. The term is critiqued by theorists like Wendy Brown who notes the implication that the "tolerated" custom or behaviour is in fact an aberrant aspect of the "other." The concern is that non interference must be limited to the private sphere and implies both the ability to punish and the conscious decision not to. This further sustains the power of dominant groups over "nonconforming" minorities. (Bill Lee)

Trans

Trans people are understood to be among the most marginalized and subjugated persons. Trans is an umbrella term that includes transsexual, transgender, transvestite and intersex persons. It is a controversial term in that it is difficult to use an umbrella term to describe all the experiences and the differing desires of trans people (Shelley, 2008). Trans gender is a contested term associated with much sophisticated theoretical development and is associated with other connections to other theoretical perspectives including feminism and queer theory. (Noble, 2006) (Ken Moffatt)

Transgender

Transgender means crossing gender. One changes gender with some sense of permanence in terms of taking up a new gender other than one's birth gender. Transgender persons can move from male to female, female to male, or take up a third or new configuration of gender. A transgendered person may transform their gender through surgery or through the manner with which they chose to live. Transgender challenges commonly accepted labels of sex, gender and sexuality. (Noble, 2006) (Ken Moffatt)

Transphobia,

Refers to the prejudice and violence experienced by people who have crossed the boundary of gender binaries. Transphobia is virulent in that it goes beyond the fear of trans persons to include attacks both verbal and physical in nature. Transphobia is also institutionalized in structures of society (including educational institutions, workplaces, medical institutions) so that trans persons are marginalized and/or excluded from social participation. (Krikorian, 2008) Although trans people often experience discrimination from family and kinship circles, in Canada trans are increasingly becoming involved in constructing families and having children. (Ken Moffatt)

Transsexual

Refers to those persons who wish to change sex. A transsexual can be either male to female or female to male. The transsexual wishes to become socially what they feel about themselves emotionally and mentally. They desire their body to conform to the expectations of the sex with which they identify. Some transsexuals engage in sexual reassignment surgery whereby they re-sex their bodies through medical sexual technologies. (Shelley, 2008)

Transvestite

A transvestite is a healthy male embodied person who dresses as a female. The transvestite most often identifies as a man. A transvestite can identify as a bisexual man, gay male, and/or a straight man. The important distinction here is that a man chooses to cross dress; that is, he dresses in clothing that is associated with women and feminine identity. There is an honoured, historical tradition of transvestite performance in LGBTTQI public spaces. (Ken Moffatt)

Values

Values are the principles considered important or desirable by an individual, group or culture. They act as guides for behaviour and allow for evaluation of our actions. Social work has a history of valuing and stating its commitment to social justice. Values inform professional codes of ethics and guide practice. A criticism of social work values is that they are influenced by humanism with an emphasis on the individual. Values such as client self determination, confidentiality, and acting in the best interest of the client support the western notion of individuality. These values may not apply to practice by and with people from cultures that focus more on the importance of community and/or extended family. Values that focus on the individual can lead to holding people personally responsible for problems that emerge as a result of social structures. Holding social justice as a primary social work value can lead to social activism, advocacy, political action, participatory research and policy development as well as individual and community interventions informed by an anti-oppressive perspective. (Sheila Sammon)

Voice

The process of people having a say about the conditions of their lives, being included as experts in defining and remedying their problems … as opposed to being unheard as more powerful 'voices' dominate and structure their lives. (Jane Aronson)

Whiteness

Recently, this term has been used to refer to the groups that dominate particularly in Western Europe and North America. Being white may not be noticed as a mark of power by the powerful because they are white. It is akin to the power of the able bodied who do not recognize their privilege over those who must navigate a society constructed by and for the able bodied. (Dumbrill, 2002: 5; New Internationalist, 2003, 18)

REFERENCES

Adamson, N., Briskin, L. and McPhail, M. (1988) *Feminist Organizing for Chang,: The Contemporary Women's Movement in Canada.* Toronto: Oxford University Press.

Alford, R.R. & Friedland R., (1985) *Powers of Theory, Capitalism, the State and Democracy,* New York: Cambridge University Press.

Alfred, T. (1999) *Peace, Power and Righteousness.* Toronto: Oxford University Press.

Alinsky, S.D. (1971) *Rules for radicals.* New York: Vintage Books.

Antone, B. Miller, D. & Myers, B. (1986) *The Power Within People.* Tribal Sovereignty Associates.

Barker, R. (1987). *The Social Work Dictionary.* Maryland: National Association of Social Workers.

Belsey, C. (2002) *Post Structuralism: A Very Short Introduction.* Oxford: Oxford University Press.

Berlin, I. (1990), *The crooked timber of humanity: Chapters in the History of Ideas,* Henry Hardy (ed.), London: John Murray; New York, 1991: Knopf.

Biever, J., Gardner, G., & Bobele, M. (1999). *"Social Construction and Narrative Family Practice".* In C. Franklin, and C. Jordan, (Eds.) *Family Practice. Brief Systems Methods for Social Work.* Pacific Grove, CA: Brooks/Cole, 143-174.

Bishop, A. (2002). *Becoming an Ally.* 2nd Edition. Halifax: Fernwood.

Bourdieu, P. (1986). The forms of capital. In J. G. Richardson (Ed.) *Handbook of theory and research for sociology of education.* Connecticut: Greenwood Press.

Brown, W. (2006) *Regulating aversion, tolerance in the age of identity and empire.* Princeton, N.J. Princeton University Press.

Brym, R. (1998*). New Society: Sociology for the 21st Century.* Toronto: Harcourt Canada, Ltd.

Bullock, A., Trombley, S. (1977), *The Fontana Dictionary of Modern Thought.* London: Collins.

Bullock, A., Trombley, S. (2002). *The New Fontana Dictionary of Modern Thought.* London: Harper Collins.

Burr, Vivien (1995). *An Introduction to Social Constructionism.* New York:: Routledge.

Canadian Oxford Dictionary (1998). Barber Katherine (Ed.) Don Mills: Oxford University Press.

Chambone, A. & Wong, F. (1999). Glossary. In Chambone, A., Irving, A. & Epstein, L. (Eds.) *Reading Foucault for Social Work.* New York: Columbia University Press, 269-280.

Cohen, H., (2003) "Deliberation and democratic legitimacy", in Matraver, D. & Pike, J. (Eds.), *Debates in Contemporary Political Philosophy.* New York: Anthology, Routledge & Open University.

Culture. www.ctcvan.ca/docs/FreedomCultural2.html.

Dominelli, L. (1998). "Anti-Oppressive Practice in Context." In Adams, R;

Dominelli, Land M. Payne (Eds) (1998). *Social Work Themes, Issues and Critical Debates.* London: Macmillan, 229-238.

Dumbrill, G. (2002*). "Child Welfare: AOP's Nemesis?"* in W. Shera (Ed.) *Emerging Perspectives on Anti-Oppressive Practice.* Toronto: Canadian Scholars Press Inc.

Eagleton, T. (2007) "Have you seen my Dada boss?" *London Review of Books*, November 30, 28(23), 9-10.

Elliott, J.L. & Fleras, A.(1992). *Unequal Relations: An Introduction to Race and Ethnic Dynamics in Canada.* Scarborough, ON: Prentice-Hall.

Fairchild, H, P. (1970). *Dictionary of Sociology and Related Sciences.* New Jersey: Littlefield, Adams, and Co.

Franklin, C. and Jordan, C.(1999). Glossary. In Franklin, C. and Jordan, C. (Eds.) *Family Practice. Brief Systems Methods for Social Work.* Pacific Grove, CA: Brooks/Cole, 427-430.

Freire, P. (2000). *Pedagogy of the Oppressed.* New York: Seabury Press.

Fung, A. & Wright, E.O., (2003) "Thinking about Empowered Participatory Governance", in Fung, A. & Wright, E.O., *Deepening Democracy.* London: Verso Books.

Garner, R. (1996). *Contemporary Movements and Ideologies.* Toronto: McGraw-Hill, Inc.

Graham, J.R. (2000). *"Diversity and Social Policy."* Canadian Social Policy: An Introduction. Prentice Hall, Inc.

Hepworth, et al. (2002*). Direct Social Work Practice: Theory and Skills.* 6th Edition. California: Brooks/Cole.

Hutchinson, A. & Lee, B. (2004). Exploring social inclusion in practice: Views from the Filed. *Canadian Social Work Review*, 22(2): 1-15.

Kaplan, A. (1996) *The development practitioners' handbook.* Chicago : Pluto Press.

Kershaw, I. (1998) *Hitler, 1889-1936, Hubris.* New York: Penguin Books.

Kilpatrick, A. and Holland, T. (1999). *Working with Families.* Boston: Allyn & Bacon.

Klein, Naomi. (2002*). Fences and Windows.* Toronto: Vintage Canada.

Krikorian, G. (2008). Transphobia (pp 468-471). In Louis- Georges Tin (ed) *The Dictionary of Homophobia, A global history of Gay and Lesbian Experience* Vancouver: Arsenal Pulp Press.

Lax, W. (1992). Postmodern Thinking in a Clinical Practice. In McNamee, S. & Gergen, K. (Eds.) *Therapy as a Social Construction.* Newbury Park, CA: Sage, 69-85.

Leckachman, R., Van Loon, B. (1981). *Capitalism For Beginners.* New York: Pantheon.

Lee, B. (1992). "Colonialization and Community: Implications for First Nations Development". *Community Development Journal.* Vol. 27, No. 3, 211-219.

Lee, B. (2001). "Case Advocacy: A Principles & Practice Guide for Social Workers and Other *Community Activists.* (Monograph) Scarborough: Nu-Spin Publications.

Lee, B. (2011) *Pragmatics of community organization.* 4th Edition. Toronto: CommonAct Press.

Lemkin, R. (1944) *Axis rule in occupied Europe: laws of occupation - analysis of government - proposals for redress.* Washington: Carnegie Endowment for International Peace, Division of International Law.

McPherson, G.R. (2009) *Resources and anthropocentrism.* Energy Bulletin, Oct. 12, http://www.energybulletin.net/50375.

Midgley, J. (1995) *Social Development: The Developmental Perspective in Social Welfare.* London: Sage Publications.

Mullaly, R. (2002). *Challenging Oppression: A Critical Social Work Approach*. Don Mills: Oxford University Press. Naming the Moment (Undated Document) Toronto: Jesuit Centre.

Noble, Jean Bobby. 2006. *Sons of the Movement, FtMs risking incoherence in a post queer cultural landscape*. Toronto: Women's Press.

Pieterse, Jan Nederveen (2001*) Development Theory: Deconstructions/Reconstructions*. Vistaar Publications: New Delhi.

Roeher Institute (1996) *Disability, Community and Society*. North York, Ont.: Roeher Institute.

Ryder, R.D. (2000) *Animal revolution: changing attitudes towards speciesism*. Berg Publishers.

Shelley, Christopher. 2008 *Transpeople: Repudiation, trauma, healing*. Toronto: University of Toronto Press.

Stiglitz, J.E. (2012) *The Price of Inequality*. New York: W.W. Norton.

Swan, T. (2003). "Anti-Oppressive Social Work Practice, Self Awareness, and the Relevance of Social Location." *Beginning to think About Anti-Oppressive Social Work*. (Monograph) In B. Lee and M. Wolfson (Eds.), 39-46.

Tracy, J. (1996) *Direct action*. Chicago: University of Chicago Press.

Wilson, M. & Whitmore, B. (2000) *Seeds of Fire: Social Development in the Era of Globalization*. Halifax NS: Fernwood.

Wolfson, M. (2002). "Examining the Territory of Structural Practice." B. Lee & M. Wolfson (Eds), *Beginning to think About Anti-Oppressive Social Work*. (Monograph), McMaster University. 17- 25.

Wong, H. (2003). "Ethnic Sensitive Social Work Models: Critical Reflections.". In B. Lee & M. Wolfson (Eds), *Beginning to think About Anti-Oppressive Social Work* (Monograph), McMaster University. 26-37.

List of Direct Contributors

Forward

Kundoqk (Jacquie Green) is from the Haisla Nation. She is the Director, School of Social Work, University of Victoria. She was the Co-Editor of the First Nations Edition, of the British Columbia Association of Social Workers. Perspectives 2003.

Definitions

Jane Aronson is the Director, School of Social Work, McMaster University, Hamilton, Ontario.

Stephanie Baker-Collins is an Associate Professor, School of Social Work, McMaster University.

Mirna E. Carranza is an Associate Professor, School of Social Work, McMaster University, Hamilton, Ontario.

Laurel Curley is an Aboriginal activist, policy analyst and part time lecturer and Ph.D. candidate at the School of Social Work, McMaster University, Hamilton, Ontario.

Janet Dassinger is a PhD candidate, School of Social Work, McMaster University.

Janet Fishlock is an international community development consultant with Planning Alliance Associates, Toronto, Ontario.

Bonnie Freeman, BA/BSW; MSW, is a Lecturer at the School of Social Work, McMaster University. Bonnie is Algonquin and Mohawk from Six Nations and is an Aboriginal activist and Ph.D. candidate, Faculty of Social Work, Wilfrid Laurier University.

Andil Gosine is an Associate Professor in the Sociology Department at York University in Toronto, Ontario.

Tony Hutchinson Ph.D. is an activist and the consultant on issues of racialized and marginalized youth. He lives in Toronto, Ontario.

Jan Johnstone MSW lives in Kincardine, Ontario, where she is a community activist and serves as a school trustee at the Bluewater District School Board.

Martha Lara is the Coordinator for Family Group Decision Making with the Children's Aid Society of Brant.

Carol LeClaire is a Red River Métis from Manitoba and an Associate Professor of Indigenous and Contemporary Studies at Wilfrid Laurier University in Brantford.

Cecelia Lee is a retired writer/researcher and editor. She lives in Toronto.

Winnie Lo is a Ph.D. candidate, McMaster University, Hamilton.

Sara Maiter is an Associate Professor, School of Social Work, York University, Toronto, Ontario.

Ken Moffatt is a Professor, Ryerson University School of Social Work, Toronto, Ontario.

Henry Parada is an Associate Professor, Ryerson University School of Social Work, Toronto, Ontario.

Meaghan Ross is a Community Development Worker at a Tenant Outreach and Education Housing Help Centre in Hamilton, Ontario.

Mac Saulis is from the Maliseet First Nation of Tobique. He was the founding Director of the Native Social Work Theme Area in the Graduate School of School of Social Work, Wilfred Laurier University, Kitchener/Waterloo, Ontario.

Katherine Schliecher, Vanessa Rankin & Michelle Gibson are graduates of the Masters of Social Work Program, School of Social Work, McMaster University, Hamilton, Ontario.

Rick Sin is a long time social worker and activist interested in issues of problems of racialization. He lives in Toronto.

Christina Sinding is an Associate Professor in the School of Social Work and the Department of Health, Aging and Society at McMaster University, Hamilton, Ontario.

Sarah Todd is an Associate Professor, Carleton University School of Social Work, Ottawa, Ontario.

June Ying Yee is an Associate professor at Ryerson University School of Social Work, Toronto, Ontario.

The Editors

Bill Lee is an Associate Professor (retired) at the School of Social Work, McMaster University. Specializing in community organization/development, Bill has worked for over 35 years as a teacher, trainer and activist in social justice causes in Canada and abroad. He is presently focusing on supporting some social justice efforts in Central America. Like Sheila Sammon he sees AOP as a journey in learning and humility.

Sheila Sammon is a Professor and chair of the Field Education Program at the School of Social Work at McMaster University. Sheila has over 25 years experience in social work education and has taught courses and workshops that address anti-oppressive perspectives. She conceptualizes learning about AOP as a journey along a path that she is still traveling.

Gary Dumbrill is an Associate Professor at McMaster University School of Social Work. Gary's research and teaching focus on child welfare, anti-oppressive practice, anti-racism and social exclusion, as well as service users' theory. Prior to joining the academy Gary was a child protection worker, first in London, England, and later in Ontario, Canada.

Research Assistant

Michelle Young BA; BSW; MSW was a most capable research assistant for the Glossary. She is presently a social worker in the Niagara Health System.